HONOLULU
is an island

Outrigger Canoe Club's Molokai race champions.

Ama'uma'u fern, Kahana Valley State Park.

Honolulu has its own fragrance.
B. J. Feldman
Former Miss Hawaii

Torch ginger, Kawailoa Plantation camp.

Pu'u Kanehoalani, Kualoa. The mountain ridge on windward Oahu named after a male ancestor of volcano goddess Pele; his female companion is said to "be" Kapapa islet in nearby Kane'ohe Bay. Kualoa, now a city park, in ancient times was considered one of the most sacred places on Oahu. When *ali'i* were in residence, passing canoes lowered their sails in recognition of his sacredness. It was also a place of refuge and is claimed by some to be the first landing place of early Polynesians on Oahu.

I think everybody is a human being no matter what land they go to. It doesn't matter. And I think if they want to come here to live, it's fine with me. And people here want to go to the mainland, which they are doing. That's fine with me. I feel that the land is created for all, even if it's said that it's only for the Hawaiians or only for the haoles or whatever. I think there's room for everybody on this land.

 Mercy Kane Harvey
 Fish merchant, Waianae

Condominium and columbarium constructed in the architectural style of two overseas cultures, share space in lower Nuʻuanu Valley.

On King Kamehameha's birthday anniversary celebration, the proud descendants of former *ali'i* dress in the colors of royalty.

Everybody is a minority here. We've learned to live, work and play together like no other place in the world . . . Honolulu gives hope to civilization that someday all of the nations on this globe will probably emulate what we have here, like tolerance of one to the other, and to me that means peace. Here, everyone is beautiful.

                      Frank Fasi, Mayor
                      Honolulu

An early morning *mauka* shower drifts *makai* across the city, from Ko'olau mountain ridges to the sea at Waikiki (overleaf).

Kalaniana'ole Highway curves along Oahu's south shore, carrying early morning commuter traffic from Hawaii Kai to downtown.

HONO
is
Photographs and Text by ROBERT WENKAM

OLULU
an island

 RAND McNALLY & COMPANY   CHICAGO • NEW YORK • SAN FRANCISCO

cknowledgement...

I wish to thank the many Honolulu residents who contributed quotations about the city they like best. Their personal comments are an important contribution. The extensive taped interviews necessary to obtain these quotations and the research, photography and writing, was made possible by financial grants from Pacific Resources, Inc., of Honolulu. This large-format, all-color book was sponsored by Pacific Resources as part of their continuing desire to present Honolulu to the world as a progressive island city and home of corporate leadership in the Pacific.

Other Books by Robert Wenkam

Hawaii The Big Island
    Photographs and text by R. Wenkam

New England
    Photographs and text by R. Wenkam

Hawaii
    Photographs and text by R. Wenkam

Micronesia: Island Wilderness
    Photographs by R. Wenkam, text by K. Brower

Maui: The Last Hawaiian Place
    Photographs and text by R. Wenkam

Micronesia: Breadfruit Revolution
    Photographs by R. Wenkam, text by B. Baker

Kauai and the Park Country of Hawaii
    Photographs and text by R. Wenkam

Editor • Herb Luthin, Chicago
Interviews for quotations • Rex Wills III, Hilo
Research • Sherry O'Sullivan, Honolulu
Design • Tom Rixford, Robert Wenkam, Honolulu
Printing and separations • R.R. Donnelley, Crawfordsville
Compositor • Boyer and Brass, San Diego
Photographs • Canon AE-1, Kodachrome 64
Production • Wenkam/Candere Publishers, Honolulu

Copyright © 1978 by Robert Wenkam   All rights reserved
Library of Congress Catalog Card Number 78-56260
International Standard Book Number: 528-81075-8
Printed in the United States of America
First printing, 1978

A corner power pole near Fernandez Village posts directions to three Saturday afternoon parties on Ewa Plantation.

Contents

Introduction To An Island • 14
Hawaiian Glossary • 19
The City Is An Island • 20
We Did It Ourselves • 27
Trees Are A Soft Green • 37
Kalakaua Boulevard Is Waikiki • 43
We Did It First • 53
Everybody's Beautiful • 60
The Islands At War • 71
We Made It A Good Town • 87
The Surf Is Up • 97
The People Who Made It So • 101
Only In Honolulu • 110
Honolulu Is Many Kinds Of Living Places • 122
The Aloha Spirit Is Not A Myth • 126

Introduction To An Island

Honolulu is possibly the world's most livable city on the most beautiful island anywhere. By federal declaration Honolulu is the cleanest, most pollution-free city of its size in the United States. A cultural and economic crossroads of the Pacific, Honolulu is the home of people of every ethnic group from everywhere and the headquarters of major international corporations. Waikiki, along with the rest of Hawaii, is by any poll the nation's most desired vacation destination. It is my favorite place to live.

We banned roadside advertising billboards 40 years ago. Hawaii has pioneered in state-wide land use laws to help preserve agricultural lands and open space. There are no unincorporated cities in Hawaii — only counties and islands — therefore we hold to a minimum wasteful economic and political competition between the legal children of the state.

Honolulu is a family place, despite the large numbers of young people who have adopted swinging contemporary lifestyles in a climate most appropriate for T-shirts, bikinis, and bare feet. It's good weather for retirement, albeit expensive, and old Asian traditions of respect for elders has been combined with the new generation's desire for independence.

We are a city of high-rise apartments and hotels that multiply at an appalling rate. It is as if they clone, because once you see two buildings, within a few years there will always be more, gradually covering the flat space between the ocean and the hills. Some have said our population density equals Hong Kong. If so, it may explain our special vitality in what is ordinarily described as the languid tropics. We are doers on a grand scale, and take full advantage of the opportunities created by city concentrations of people and conveniently located Waikiki, which free-spending tourists have created for us. Honolulu affords a symphony, great art collections, a magnificent Pacific museum, community theaters, and a concert hall, where popular entertainers regularly stop off on their way to somewhere else.

We created our urban environment, and it satisfies our personal needs very well; therefore, is it not exactly what we want? Some say that urban design is a political art form, that our city was created in the political arena. Not so. Our politicians merely responded to the most powerful and influential economic pressures — the landowners and the businessmen that in contemporary Honolulu seem to have consistently acted in concert with the long-range best interests of the community. Even when their profit-motivated actions took priority, the end result was positive. The importation of foreign plantation workers and the expansion of monopolistic corporate land holdings are probably more responsible for the Honolulu of today than any other factor.

We created an urban package within our island state and added political appendages that further enhanced its livability. There are no separate school districts in Hawaii, or expensive property assessments to support them — all students, rich and poor, receive education funds on an equal basis from state funds. There is no state police (despite the myth of "Hawaii Five-O"), but there are excellent state library and hospital systems. Honolulu and Hawaii, by any measure a racially and economically divided community 20 years ago, solved most of its social problems before the federal civil rights act became the law of the land — and before Hawaii became the fiftieth state.

Honolulu is also a fragile city. Resting lightly between pleasantly green hills and the incredibly blue ocean, floating beneath a sky never dulled by smog (not yet), the island environment is easily damaged by too many people — residents or visitors. The danger is not just rhetoric by environmentalists. It is official government policy to be concerned about Hawaii's growth rate and population. The governor said so in his state of the state message. The legislature has passed a general plan policy statement that addresses itself to the problem of too many people on too small an island. Legislators have

I started out in Kalihi, when I was a youngster. Then I growed up in Kapahulu near Waikiki. In those days Waikiki was a nice place, back in the fifties, when I was a teenager, you know. There's too much building there now. The way the buildings went up overnight, yeah? Although I'm a construction worker myself, I hope this doesn't happen to the other islands — like Waikiki and stuff like that, huh? . . . And a lot of transients, yeah? Y'know Waikiki doesn't have the feeling of old Hawaii, but the young local people there are trying to bring it back I believe. I think they're getting successful now, because there's more Hawaiians and local people that are taking interest in their culture now. And that's important. You gotta hang onto some of the past because you gotta identify where you come from, eh?

*Keala Brown
Bulldozer operator, Kaneohe*

also requested the state Department of Transportation to determine how many automobiles can drive around the island at any one time.

The state Department of Planning and Economic Development has also tried to determine how many people is too many, again without success. Environmental groups generally agree there are too many already. Even the tourist industry has agreed on the maximum number of rooms Waikiki can absorb and still be a nice place for tourists; it encouraged passing of city ordinances that offer certain combinations of density and setback, and which would eventually limit rooms in Waikiki to about 29,000 — only 6,000 more than today's count.

Continued growth of Honolulu is a statistical nightmare. Computer projections, based on the last ten years of tourist growth rate, forecast very good business for the tourist industry 100 years from today, when 60 trillion, 450 billion tourists will arrive at the airport every hour! Perhaps such projections are absurb, but if so, the reckless economic philosophy of growth ad infinitum must be seriously questioned.

The Hawaii Visitors Bureau estimates that almost four million tourists visited Hawaii in 1978, most of them spending all of their vacation in Honolulu and leaving behind for the Hawaii economy over a billion dollars in circulating cash. Most tourists returned home satisfied with happy memories, but many remained because they liked living here better than at home. Many more flew over to work in fancy resorts and live like others dream. Some deplaned at the Honolulu airport and next day rode TheBus to the downtown welfare office — when they learned it is difficult to hold a job while surfing all day.

M ost island residents are well aware there is no legal way to restrict immigration, as there is implied in Governor Ariyoshi's declared concern over population. As Herbert Cornuelle, president of Dillingham Corporation, says, "It would have been very nice to be able to pull up the drawbridge just after I arrived in Honolulu in 1953, but that's not possible."

"I can see what the governor is talking about, but I can't be against immigration," asserts Cornuelle. "The essence of everything the U.S. and Hawaii is — is based on people coming here from everywhere. And here is the one place that certainly epitomizes that you've been wel-

On Kalakaua Boulevard in Waikiki, the surf is up.

come, rich or poor, no matter what color, and I don't want to change that. I like that idea and I don't see why we would want to pull up the drawbridge."

Mainlanders, sick of street crime, prejudice, and pollution of their air and water, clamor for escape to Hawaii. The island paradise created by travel pundits is still the end of the rainbow despite a few tarnished hues. Never mind that Aloha Week is celebrated with plastic leis from Hong Kong and that the "fresh" *mahimahi* on hotel menus is mostly shipped frozen from Taiwan. So what if the Polynesian pageantry is fake and ancient torches burn propane. The rainbows and flowers and surf are real. The clean sky s real. So is the scenery, the beautiful people, and the soft landscape seemingly ever green. The sun is interrupted only momentarily by passing showers. Every day is a sleepy Sunday, and even the winter week is a shirt-sleeved summer. Is it any wonder the world wants to crop by and stay? ■

If you can't say anything good about anybody don't say anything at all.

Yvonne Elliman
Honolulu born vocalist

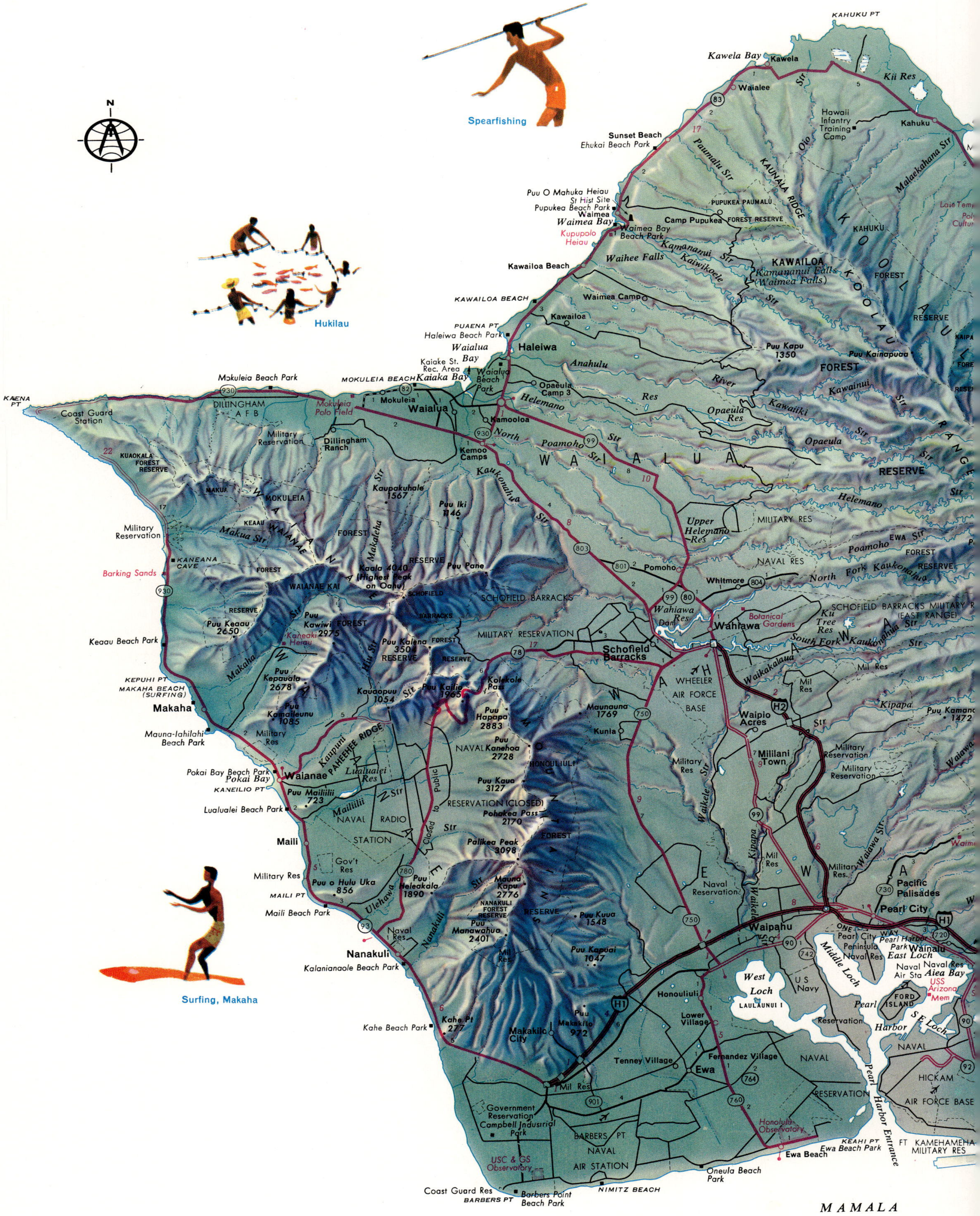

Spearfishing

Hukilau

Surfing, Makaha

Ilima, Flower of Oahu

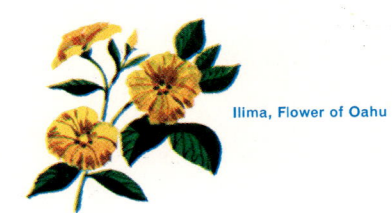

"We are still unique — we are still ourselves — we are still Polynesia."
Commentary at Polynesian Cultural Center, La'ie.

Hawaiian Glossary

The earliest known list of Hawaiian words is in Captain Cook's account of his explorations compiled in 1778, the year of Cook's discovery of the Sandwich Islands. Two hundred years later we have compiled another list, the shortest of all lists, to enable readers to better understand Hawaiian words not defined in the text.

Reverend Lorenzo Lyons wrote in 1878 that the Hawaiian language "is one of the oldest living languages of the earth, as some conjecture, and may well be classed among the best... The thought to displace it, or doom it to oblivion by substituting the English language, ought not for a moment be indulged." We agree and we prefer not to substitute where Hawaiian words have become part of our vocabulary. It is for this reason that anyone can quickly recognize a *kama'aina*, for their English will be well sprinkled with Hawaiian words fondly adopted over the years.

The Hawaiian language, first compiled by the missionaries after their arrival in 1820, has changed little, but dictionaries and the printed form have changed from time to time, and in this book we have used the presentation that most clearly reveals the correct spelling and proper way to pronounce even the most complex words. Glottal stop marks are used throughout; but for reasons of clarity in reading, we have dropped the hyphen, and I hope the linguists will forgive us. All that we know is derived from the *Hawaiian-English Dictionary* by Mary Kawena Pukui and Samuel H. Ebert (University of Hawaii Press).

I cannot explain how to pronounce Hawaiian, except to suggest the reader try to pronounce words the way they are spelled (I understand a knowledge of Latin helps). Pronounce each vowel as a separate syllable, with accent on the next to last syllable. Vowels are pronounced like *a* in above, *e* in bet, *i* in city, *o* in sole, and *u* like in moon. Don't worry too much about *w*. Most of the time, give it a very slight *v* sound. To further aid in pronouncing words with multiple vowels, we have included the glottal stop, which is similar to the sound between the *oh's* in English *oh-oh*.

Now practice on *Ka'a'awa*, a small community on Oahu's windward shore. Being able to pronounce Hawaiian the way it sounds greatly enhances the pleasure of reading about Hawaii. ■

Ahupua'a • Land division
Akua • Powerful god
Ala Moana • Road by the sea
Ala Wai • Canal
Ali'i • Royalty
Aloha • Love, greeting
Aumakua • Family Gods
Hale • House
Hana • Work
Haole • White person
Hau'oli • Happiness
Heiau • Pre-Christian place of worship
Ho'omalimali • To flatter
Hulihuli • Turning repeatedly
Iki • Small
Kama'aina • Born in Hawaii
Kanaka • Hawaiian, person
Kane • Man
Kapakahi • Crooked
Kapu • Forbidden
Kaukau • Food
Kepani • Japanese
Kihapai • Garden patch
Kuhina nui • Prime minister
Lanai • Porch
Lani • Sky
Lei • Flower garland
Lililili • Extreme jealousy
Limu • Seaweed
Lua • Outhouse
Luau • Hawaiian feast
Luna • Supervisor
Mahalo • Thank you
Makahiki • Year, festival
Makai • Toward the sea
Make • Dead
Malihini • Newcomer
Mana • Supernatural power
Mauka • Toward the mountains
Mauna • Mountain
Mele • Chant
Menehune • Hawaiian gnome
Moana • Ocean
Mu'umu'u • Loose covering dress
Nui • Large
'Ono • Delicious
Pake • Chinese
Pali • Cliff
Papale • Hat
Pau • Ended
Piko • Navel
Pilikia • Trouble
Pua'a • Pig
Puka • Hole
Pukiki • Portuguese
Pupule • Crazy
Pu'u • Mountain peak
'Ukulele • Leaping flea
Wahine • Woman
Wikiwiki • Quick

The City Is An Island

At dawn a faint glow appears. Flying over Oahu, two miles above the sleeping city, the first light is without any color. Next, the glow is pink, laid below a fuzzy purple band against the gray darkness next to the black sky overhead. At this early hour only the stars give dimension to space beyond, a space gradually evolving to deep blue as the sun appears, at one point matching the ocean's perpetual blue when the sea blends into the sky and the horizon disappears.

At sea level, when the ocean accepts the dark blue of the sky at daylight, the dawn is dark gray at first, gradually changing into warm magenta hues, then pink and orange as the earth spins eastward and the ocean waves approaching the island reflect a first glimmer of light into Waikiki hotel rooms to leeward.

The day begins earlier for windward dwellers on the east side of Oahu, where the sun rises from beneath the ocean and shines directly into panoramic-view windows of suburban homes perched on low hills below the *pali* and above the sea. It is breakfast time for windward people.

Across the island, on the other side, away from the rising sun in the morning shadow of Koʻolau peaks, gray rain clouds spread outward over the still drowsy city, sprinkling streets with brief rain showers drifting *makai*. The air is sweet and still moist in the cool of early morning. It is twilight at dawn until the sun is high enough to burn back the clouds before sweeping downward onto the leeward shore, drying wet streets now gradually filling with mixed clutches of trucks, cars and the mayor's yellow buses (TheBus), all pouring together into downtown like colored sand draining from a glass funnel. It is not until later in the morning before the sun rises full over the city. Leeward people never see a sunrise in bed.

Honolulu is a skinny city, stretched out like some lazy hound dog relaxing on the beach with his paws in the water at Waikiki and long ears flopped against the green hills that in valley and ridge repeat the curves of the shoreline. The tail wags in Hawaii Kai and the tongue laps Pearl Harbor. Urban planners say it is the perfect kind of city for a fixed-guideway mass transit system.

Urban Honolulu has no main street that can be clearly identified. The town just rambles on all over. The old cow paths that eventually became boulevards apparently went only as far as the feeding trough. Kalakaua, Kapiolani, and Fort streets seem to end before they really get anywhere. Only Lunalilo Freeway squirms boldly through Honolulu between old residential areas and new condominiums, from its beginning in Kahala to its grand slam finish at Aloha Stadium, where it disperses rapidly into a maze of interstate interchanges.

Honolulu was not platted in square blocks like San Francisco or provided with wide boulevards like Paris. Nothing seems planned nor premeditated. The whole thing just grew, and continues to expand in the same unorganized pattern that somehow reflects the informality of its lifestyle. It defies the traffic engineer's logic. Improving traffic flow is like diverting a freeway through an ant hill, and as automobiles have steadily increased in this long, narrow city, conversion of many streets into one-way routes became the only solution. Driving home at times is best accomplished by continuing straight ahead around the island. Honolulu may be the only city where any direction is the way home.

The island is small. Kamehameha Highway, the only round-the-island road, is just 94 miles from the beginning and back. At the narrow part a two-hour hike to summit ridges offers a view of both sides of the island at once. It is difficult to believe that Oahu boasts 52 miles of the U.S. Interstate Highway System, with only one gap between Honolulu and the nearest stub in southern California. Eighty-two percent of the state's population of over 800,000 live in Honolulu, and these 656,000 people drive over 300,000 automobiles!

Half an hour from downtown by interstate freeway, north beyond Pearl Harbor, the city flattens out into a soft carpet of green sugarcane covering fertile plains between the Koʻolau and Waiʻanae mountains. The twin mountain ranges, extending northwesterly, effectively interrupt trade wind patterns and force most of Oahu's rain to fall on windward slopes, leaving leeward shores sunny and dry. Honolulu and Waikiki seldom experience heavy rain — it is mostly "liquid sunshine," as defined in tourist advertising; mostly a misty drizzle falling lazily from broken cumulus sailing with the wind as the clouds break away from clinging hills. It is a rain that reflects rainbows across the city, and why there is a greater difference in rainfall between windward and leeward sides of the island than between summer and

---

The ocean path of the setting sun intercepts a schooner in Mamala Bay off Honolulu Harbor. Mamala was a shark woman in Hawaiian lore who lived at the entrance to Honolulu Harbor and often played *konane,* an ancient game resembling checkers.

winter. When the city forgets to pick up after itself, a night rain washes the dust away.

Honolulu is basic green, blue, and white — the colors of the mountains, the sea, and the sky. The space surrounding the green hills is blue. It is delineated by the highest ridge and softened by *mauka* showers moving slowly across the city. The rain falls from white cumulus clouds that define wind direction and strength, breaking away from the mountaintops in long clusters that cling to the hills briefly before letting go and bringing to the city moisture, shade, and coolness.

White buildings dominate the skyline like a sharp, serrated knife on edge, hugging the surf line like a crownflower *lei* thrown into the sea, and having floated back to shore, is caught in the ceaseless sweep of waves upon the land.

Only a close look reveals other colors. They appear on people and flowers, seldom on homes and buildings, but they blend well into the Hawaii landscape. Only the blue, green and white have always been here. Everything else is an immigrant from another continent, brought here by birds, waves, and early travelers to become a botanical Pandora's box that in this case is a pleasure to open.

The city is trimmed in white, the hue of almost everything man has made. No cold season interrupts the perpetual spring to change the basic color of things. All year the hills behind the city are green, washed clean by the evening rain. The city is as if built upon a magnificent natural stage, with the evergreen mountains its contrasting, never-wilting backdrop. The clouds are a proscenium arch bridging the sky, bringing mountain summits to the sea in one unbroken spatial grasp, giving visual unity to the city, and locating it stage center. Onstage, and outlining the green mountain shape with the random heights of urban shapes, are angular buildings and small white houses scattered among the high-rise apartments where man encroaches upon nature. The director is creating another scene.

Early Hawaiians had words for all these spaces, shapes, and places. The circle of sky extending from the horizon they called *kahiki-ku*. The space overhead was *luna-a'e*; the space between the heavens and the earth was sometimes called *kalewa*. Where the birds fly is *lewa-nu'u*.

The Hawaiian's close relationship to and dependence upon the physical world — land, sea, and sky — evolved into a language that reflected this relationship. With an unwritten vocabulary, and with word nuances perfectly suited to island needs, they understood the spiritual significance of the shape of spaces, and they defined spaces that have no equivalent in English. Who else has defined the space below where a person would swing from a tree with his feet clear of the ground? The space is *lewa ho'omakua*. And the space beneath where we stand — *lalo*.

Perhaps the island lifestyle and the easy-going human relationships are indeed inherited from our Hawaiian ancestors on some cultural bridge. To some extent, we are indebted to their keen understanding of the spaces around us and how it affects our daily lives. It is well known that we determine what we build and in turn are shaped by the World we build. Are we island people the way we are because we are on an island, and are conscious of the space around us that extends beyond where we can see?

Hawaiians called this space *kukulu-o-kahonua*, the compass of the earth. When it is understood that our physical world has its limits, when we can see both sides of the island that is our home, it may be easier to satisfy human relationships that clearly cannot be escaped.

Honolulu has experienced a cultural, economic, and social revolution since the end of World War II that has substantially changed the people, the land, and the economy. Yet in many ways Honolulu has not changed at all. With all the attributes of a big city, it is still much like a small town, with all the pleasant things a small town has to offer. Honolulu has made the quantum leap from an oligarchic plantation town into a sophisticated contemporary city with little pain and discomfort, without becoming hard and selfish. Somehow, the better characteristics of a small place were retained while adapting the economic advantages and cultural wealth of a big city.

Our pleasant, permissive weather obviously helped to keep dress styles informal; but positive humanitarian values also prevailed, even when opposing sides both had a battle to win. Under similar circumstances elsewhere, violence was often the answer to difficult controversy. Exceptions can be found, but in the years that Hawaii rapidly grew into a democratic community, creating in the process a prosperous middle class where none existed before, the incidents of violent confrontation scarcely rate a mention when measured against the major accomplishments that are the result of compromise and evenhanded judgement.

Somehow we grew up without fighting each other — without the remnants of hate and bitterness that plague so many world communities. Is it because we live upon an island? ■

In the hills above Oahu's urban tangle, a tropical forest surrounds Sunday afternoon hikers on a Hawaiian Trail & Mountain Club hike on the Honouliuli trail, Wai'anae Mountains.

Kamehameha's conquering army pushed Oahu's warriors over the *pali* in upper Nu'uanu Valley. The scenic view was later saved from subdividers by Hawaii's unique land use law (overleaf).

We Did It Ourselves

It required over seven centuries for the people of Hawaii to make these islands the place they are today — for the early Polynesians to find Hawaii and begin changing the landscape. They first investigated New Zealand to the south in voyages from the Tahiti area before sailing northward and settling into the several islands they called Hawaii. They apparently liked Hawaii and decided to stay here because there is no evidence they sailed any further to investigate the mainland, although these early sailors did have the necessary navigational skills and seaworthy double-hulled canoes to explore colder waters should anyone have desired. They adapted Polynesian living styles to their newly discovered home and settled down permanently to create the Hawaiian nation.

Women stepped ashore with the men, carrying seeds of edible fruits and medicinal plants, coconuts, breadfruit, taro, and sugarcane, bringing pigs and dogs, along with a spoken language, warriors, and *ali'i* — the cultural grafts for the new civilization that began in Hawaii about 700 years ago. Within 500 years their highest *ali'i*, Kamehameha, with the help of Western cannon and gunpowder, conquered all the islands and crowned himself king. Hawaii was possibly the last place on earth to be discovered and settled, although conquering is still going on elsewhere.

British Captain Cook followed long after the first Polynesian arrivals, navigating with sailing instructions given the explorer by the king of Tahiti. Cook sailed straight northward to Hawaii after leaving Tahiti, with only one stop enroute at Christmas Island over the holidays, where his ships were restocked with water and coconuts. Missionaries arrived in Hawaii some 50 years later, and they were appropriate precursors to the whalers and later merchant shippers, who introduced agricultural crops for export and established a plantation system that required the import of indentured labor from around the world. The land was fertile, with ample water, plentiful fish, and abundant natural resources; but if all this bounty was to last — to feed, house, and clothe a growing population — the land must be properly cared for.

The ruling Hawaiian *ali'i* called his unique land subdivisions *ahupua'a*, and specifically located boundaries to include differing land uses, thereby providing for all his people's needs within his own feudal domain, and incidentally making it much easier to collect taxes.

Feathers, canoe logs, and spears came from the mountains; taro, bananas, and sweet potatoes from the lowlands; fish and seaweed from the sea. Waters outside coral reefs were assigned to commoners; those between reefs and beach, to *ali'i*. The beach was unassigned and available to all. To this day, the beach between the high-water mark and the sea remains public.

It is said that in ancient times whenever a canoe log was cut in the high forest the ground was prepared for another tree to be planted in its place. And that collectors of feathers for the magnificent royal capes took only individual feathers and let the bird fly free. Even in later years a land lease granted by King Kamehameha's commissioner of public lands included the admonishment not to "permit or suffer to be done, any willful or voluntary waste, spoil or destruction. . . ." Conservation is indeed a tradition in Hawaii, a tradition adopted in kind by immigrants from other lands as their political and economic influence gradually become effective. The plantation manager, taro farmer, and resort developer all seemed to possess some kind of innate concern for preservation and protection of the land.

Cruel scars on the landscape, a legacy of 200 years of

Of all the cities in the United States as measured by five polluting elements being monitored in the atmosphere by government agencies, Honolulu is the only major city with a clean bill of health. Every other city is deficient in at least one category of pollution. Honolulu is the cleanest city of its size in the nation.

I've been involved in the kind of life in the last few years where I've had to be gone a great deal, and it gets a little frustrating because all I want to do is spend more time in Hawaii. When the plane lands at Honolulu airport (and it's usually midnight or one o'clock in the morning) and they open that door and that soft Hawaiian air comes in — it's one of the greatest feelings in the world.

James F. Gary, President
Pacific Resources, Inc.

Bertram Street on hilly St. Louis Heights, glistens in passing showers, bringing a rainbow to Waikiki, far below in the wet sunlight.

Sixty thousand people can sleep overnight in Waikiki. Only a few hundred will find room on crowded Waikiki Beach during daylight hours, but there will always be room for yellow bikinis.

intensive use since Cook sailed into Kealakekua Bay, are ample evidence that Hawaii has been sometimes treated roughly; but these scars seem less an overall indictment than a way of measuring the great beauty still remaining, even on Oahu where urbanization seems overwhelming. One of the problems in identifying environmental progress is that success may be vacant lots or farmland everyone takes for granted — as if it had always been there and always will be there. Defeat is a concrete highrise monument we face every day.

It is difficult to imagine the streets of 60 years ago, when billboards hawking catsup, tamales, and whiskey blocked the view of Diamond Head. A giant green pickle was appliquéd across the *pali*, and on the slopes of Punchbowl white letters ten feet high advertised soap. Prime scenic areas were tacky with mammoth signs promoting everything from Bull Durham "roll your own" to patent medicines and chewing gum.

Forty advertisers were effectively blotting out choice portions of the scenery when a determined group of Honolulu women organized the Outdoor Circle to promote civic betterment, and specifically "to rid the city of billboards."

When it was learned their club treasury did not have sufficient moneys to buy the billboard companies, the women launched a city-wide boycott, urging the public not to use advertised goods, and directly challenged downtown merchants to stop advertising. They were the first to enlist the Honolulu Chamber of Commerce in a conservation campaign. The new Hawaii "tourist" bureau unanimously endorsed the women's campaign and the old Honolulu Board of Supervisors voted its support. It was the beginning of cooperation among environmentalists, businessmen, and politicians to keep Hawaii beautiful.

After 14 years of boycott and refusal to compromise on decorative smaller signs, only chewing gum and cigarettes remained on the billboards. Local firms had long since canceled their advertising, and there was little business left for the single remaining company; it agreed to sell when the women again offered to buy the last billboards. They successfully raised the money and for one week became the only conservation organization in the outdoor advertising business. Outstanding contracts were quickly canceled and the termite-infested boards dismantled and burned. Diamond Head could be seen again from Honolulu's open-air streetcars crossing the McCully Street Bridge. The next year, legislation was enacted outlawing billboards in Hawaii.

Struggles between development, economic growth, and environmental protection raged constantly in every state legislative session, in every meeting of the Board of Supervisors, and more recently in the Honolulu City Council as well. But as the battles raged, protagonists on the side of preserving Hawaii's natural scenic resources, open space, and the island environment gathered together unusual allies that did not occur elsewhere. In the confrontation over saving Diamond Head — to halt construction of high-rise hotels on the famous landmark — Honolulu councilmen advocating "growth and progress" and more hotels, were opposed by the Sierra Club, Chamber of Commerce, Conservation Council of Hawaii, AFL construction trade unions, and the Oahu Development Conference, a planning group sponsored by the largest corporations in Honolulu. Diamond Head won.

Environmental controversies extended over many years, even during the time of the Republic of Hawaii and territorial days. When sugar and pineapple interests generally prevailed over all else, concern over the land and its proper use was always given serious consideration at all government levels. Many compromises were made, many unfortunate plans were approved, and permanent scars were imposed upon the land, like Interstate TH-3 cutting the heart out of Puʻu Papaʻa on its spear-straight route to Kaneohe; but overall, most of the decisions

Article VIII
PUBLIC SIGHTLINESS AND GOOD ORDER SECTION 5.
The State shall have power to conserve and develop its natural beauty, objects and places of historic or cultural interest, sightliness and physical good order, and for that purpose private property shall be subject to reasonable regulation.
The Constitution of the State of Hawaii

seemed to be the correct ones. Somehow we saved more than we lost, and what we did save was the most important.

Probably the most significant legislation passed by any state is Hawaii's progressive land use law, which provides for state zoning and management of all public and private lands in the state. Supported by another unusual coalition of citizen conservationists, businessmen, and large landowners, the unique law was enacted to slow down urban sprawl, to halt rising farmland taxes, and to end speculative manipulation of agricultural lands. Like any law, implementation by appointed administrators has determined how effective it is; but much of the natural beauty and open space of today's Hawaii is a testimonial to the land use law's effectiveness, despite attempts to repeal made in every legislative session by county governments demanding a return to "home rule."

The late Governor John Burns fully supported the law and also urged the use of the legislation to protect scenic beauty, as well as sugar and pineapple lands, arguing that both are of equal importance to the state's economy and deserve equal protection. In a talk before the Conservation Council of Hawaii, he said, "We have the basic land use law on our books to protect and enhance Hawaii's resources of scenic beauty and open spaces. . . . Ownership of land does not carry with it the right to deface its natural beauty in the name of progress." I had written that speech for the governor, along with many others on conservation that were given during his successful campaign.

Dole pineapple, Wahiawa Plantation.

In his first month of office, Governor Burns appointed me a State Land Use Commissioner. My first thought was to take whatever action necessary to reverse the usual priorities that favored development over everything else. As for me, "conservation" zoning was far more important to the future of these islands than expansion of urban land uses. One-half of all land in Hawaii is now zoned "conservation" and given the state's strongest protection against unwise short-term uses and destructive development. It's not permanent protection, but it's better than any other state offers. The ancient *ali'i* had actually taken the preparatory action hundreds of years before when they divided their *ahupua'a* into primitive land use districts. We just updated the old Hawaiian system.

Protection of the land is the law of the land in Hawaii. A total ban on billboards, state-wide land zoning, a restrictive business sign ordinance for Honolulu, a protective coastal zone act, creation of a general plan for the state, and even establishment of specific tourist destination areas backed up by the land use law, all are demonstrative of the people's determination to grow and prosper while conserving the island environment. The people of Hawaii, through their elected representatives and appointed commissioners, have been able to play a role in creating the Hawaii seen today.

As in any working democratic relationship, compromise has been the name of the political game. Political corruption is not unknown. The ownership of land still carries most of the traditional constitutional rights of development, speculation, and profit. But the history of Hawaii and Honolulu — and of the scenic beauty around us — is surely ample evidence of the fact that concern for our land and the island environment is an integral part of our island lifestyle.

Most of Hawaii's politicians hold to the usual free-enterprise economic thinking: that growth is good and that development is to be encouraged, "to make jobs" and "to provide a larger tax base for the city;" but their final votes, even after checking with campaign contributors, generally seem to be tempered by thoughts of how their decisions will affect our environment. If elected legislators are a bit slow in recognizing this concern, a veritable army of active citizen environmentalists reminds them. During the campaign to stop high-rise hotel construction on the front profile of Diamond Head, over 35 community organizations joined together to convince wavering city councilmen that their political future was in jeopardy if the famed landmark's profile was to be desecrated with hotels. The candidate for mayor who thought it proper to build a few hotels on Diamond Head was defeated. Frank Fasi, who won, appointed a conservationist chairman of his Advisory Committee to Save Diamond Head. No hotels were built and the land was up-zoned to park and to open space.

There have been a few losses. Developers filled in Salt Lake, the only large natural lake on Oahu, to build a golf course. Twenty years ago we tried to convert Kalakaua Boulevard into a pedestrian mall, but Waikiki property owners were able to convince city politicians otherwise. We haven't been able to stop the continuing urbanization of caneland around Pearl Harbor, nor strip development of Kamehameha Highway on the north shore; but we did stop the rampaging transportation planners from going ahead with ill-advised schemes for freeways on offshore reefs, for a double-decked interstate *makai* freeway to cover Ala Moana Boulevard and the waterfront, and for another spur of the interstate through beautiful and historical Moanalua Valley — the TH-3 to Kaneʻohe.

Hotels planned for Magic Island and Ala Moana Park were never built. I remember walking to then-Governor Burn's office and being shown several elaborate color renderings of hotels to be built in the park, "to help pay for the park." I took one look at the plans and assured the governor that every citizens group in the city would oppose this scheme, and that he would be well advised to have nothing to do with hotels on Magic Island. After a short discussion he agreed and stacked the drawings against the wall behind his desk. They were never released to the press, and the hotels were never built.

When Standard Oil of California came to town a few years back, announcing plans to construct a major oil refinery on Sand Island in Honolulu Harbor, within one mile of downtown Fort Street, the general public was outraged. Especially when Standard insisted that Sand Island was the only possible site and threatened to cancel the project, with all its promised jobs, if they were not granted permission to build where it wanted to build — in Honolulu Harbor. Full-page ads financed by philanthropist and Bishop Estate Trustee Atherton Richards helped convince Standard Oil that the industrial park at Barbers Point on Campbell Estate lands would be a better location.

When I joined the state Land Use Commission, the privately owned Castle Ranch lands below the Nuʻuanu Pali viewpoint were already subdivided on paper. Engineering drawings were completed, streets named, and preliminary subdivision approval granted by the city. I immediately went to work to stop the subdivision that would destroy forever one of Hawaii's famed scenic views. Land use conservation district regulations prohibited subdivisions, so it was my intent to have the land zoned "conservation," to make it possible for existing dairy pasture and banana farms to remain and benefit from lower property tax assessments.

I traded votes wherever necessary with my fellow commissioners to obtain a unanimous vote to zone all the *pali*-view lands as "conservation." There are controversial subdivisions on all the outside islands that benefitted from my "yes" votes to obtain a "no" vote for subdividing Castle Ranch lands. It was a practical example of legislative democracy at work, to achieve a community goal that benefitted the long-range best interests of everyone.

Hawaii didn't get to be the "most beautiful islands anchored in any ocean" by accident. We did it this way quite deliberately — from the very beginning. We learned from everywhere. From the early German forester who carried water on mules into the Waiʻanaes to water his seedlings, planted by hand. A stroll on the Honouliuli trail proves his effort at reforestation was quite worthwhile. When sugar planters overthrew the monarchy to assure their valuable crop entry into the profitable American market, they also established a state forest reserve system on private lands to protect their watershed. It thrives to this day — there are no federal forest lands in Hawaii.

Even the monopolistic plantations and large estates, which together own and control most of the land in Hawaii, played a role in preserving, intact, extensive agricultural lands — it was not necessary for them to sell off bits and pieces like smaller property owners. The great unbroken expanses of cane and pineapple growing on the uplands of Oahu still preserve visual open space between the mountains and the sea that continue to make a drive to the north shore from downtown an unusual spiritual experience. Crossing Oahu to the other side is to verify again the limits of our island home, and to confirm that this finite geography is what probably gave us the concern for its care and protection. Our immigrants from everywhere gave us the skills to do so. ■

People are happy here because of comparisons. We may get a little worse over the years, but compared to every other place we're better. The gap between us and the rest of the world, if anything, has widened. We're better compared to them.

Herbert Cornuelle, President
Dillingham Corporation

Young *keiki* from Kapiʻolani Butterworth's Hula Studio dance for Sunday visitors and residents at the vast Ala Moana Shopping Center.

Honolulu is one of the prettiest cities in the world. I have been to 67 countries in my life and I have never seen a city that has as attractive downtown area as this one, and it's continuously improving. Going back 30 or 40 years I can remember the downtown areas and the city was not pretty. Somehow, gradually, with the redevelopment that has taken place in downtown, with the big, broad highways that go up through the valleys, which I think add to the beauty of the city because people can enjoy the beauty of the city, because people can enjoy the beauty from the Pali Highway, from Likelike Highway — Honolulu has indeed become a very beautiful city.

The aloha spirit obviously gets diluted as we get more and more mainland people here. The core of Hawaiians and old-time residents obviously is smaller in proportion to the total population, but Honolulu does have a spirit. It does have a feeling all of its own. And I think that people who come here and stay for a time become imbued with that feeling. Of course, there are exceptions, but I know all sorts of people who've moved here from far away and have taken Hawaii as their own. And I think that's very definitely true with Honolulu, and one of the reasons that Hawaii is a nice place to live. Some of these people have built the Honolulu we know today.

I think that all the companies in Hawaii, for obvious reasons, are searching out competent women, are searching out competent personnel from minority races. I don't think a double standard is really a problem here, because in the first place we don't really have any minority races. However, in the old days there was unquestionable bias against Orientals. That has long since passed. Some of the more competent people, perhaps some of the most competent people in this company, are Orientals. Some of the most competent people I know of in Hawaiian business are Orientals. The old days of bias have not only passed, but are well past. . . . I'm very proud of the fact that I actually made the motion to admit the first citizen of Japanese ancestry into the Pacific Club some years ago. That is all in the past and it's a good thing.

Honolulu is more than just a place — it's a state of mind. It's a particularly beautiful place and state of mind combined. It's beautiful because it is racially harmonic — as racially harmonic as a place in this "state of change" can be. It has this happiness halfway between the Orient and the West. It has the mixture of Polynesia, of Asia, of the Europeans — all put together in one location. And I think that makes a super mixture. A super kind of place that only happens once in the world and it's happened here.

Henry A. Walker, Jr., Chairman
Amfac, Inc.

The financial center of downtown Honolulu surrounds Bishop Street, named after Charles Reed Bishop, early financier and public official who married Princess Bernice Pauahi and established the Bishop Museum in her honor. Bishop Street was cut through their old home site.

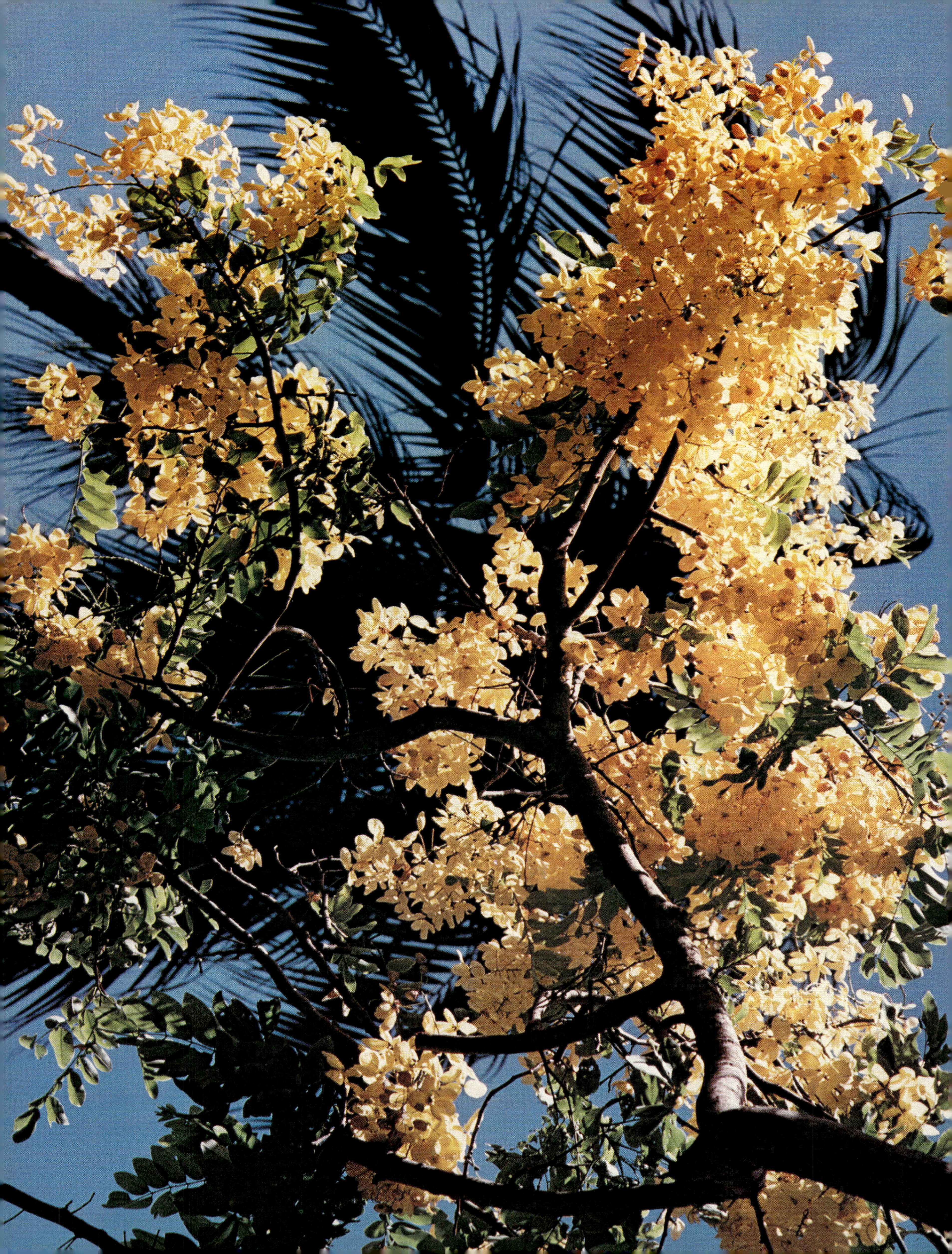

Trees Are A Soft Green

Trees are green. Lots of them are a distinguishing feature of Honolulu where shaded tunnels on residential streets are nostalgic reminders of another era when the horse and carriage always traveled a tree-lined path. Today new apartment towers stand high above the blanket of green softly covering older sections of the city, gracefully wrapping urban space between the mountains and the sea.

It is quite evident from viewing old photographs that Hawaii has many more trees than say, a hundred years ago, but it might be debatable whether we have more trees today than twenty years ago. For awhile, during the post-statehood building boom, we may have been cutting urban trees faster than they grew. The community did object, as they always have been very protective of trees in Honolulu, but the economic pressures of "growth and progress" often overwhelmed even the best intentioned city official. A previous administration actually sent out workers in pre-dawn raids to cut down more controversial trees, so it would be too late for conservationists to seriously object after the denuded streets were discovered.

In the days before accountants kept tabs on expenses, plantation managers would on occasion divert a few field hands from sugar growing to tree planting. The magnificent exotic trees shading Kemo'o Road to Waialua are part of this heritage. Wives of these same sugar executives joined downtown women in organizing the Outdoor Circle 65 years ago to augment rural planting and bring some greenery into the city. Half a century ago, Honolulu hillsides were bare and dry, with more cactus than grass, much of the desolation due to overgrazing by goats and a general die-back of sensitive native plants and grasses.

Writing in the *Historic Hawaii News*, Dorothy Hargreaves tells of the first planting by Outdoor Circle women in A'ala Park, Honolulu's earliest public playground. The women planted 28 monkeypod trees, which now offer a continuous shaded canopy surrounding the grassed play area. The Circle women also planted coconut palms along Kalakaua Avenue in Waikiki; the rows of mahogany trees between Beretania and Kapi'olani; and miles of colorful shower trees on highways and residential streets. These trees have all grown into mature specimens that in some cases have spread across the street from curb to curb, creating great gothic arches of green that considerably enhance the city. The more than 280 ironwood trees *(casuarina equisetifolia)* in Kapi'olani Park were planted in 1890 by A. S. Cleghorn, father of Princess Kaiulani.

Several trees over 100 years old grow on the Castle Ranch behind Olomanu. Here is a large Norfolk Island pine *(Araucaria)*, where Queen Lilioukalani is said to have composed "Aloha Oe," and a double row of 30 royal palms still lining the old carriage road used by royalty in the days of the kingdom. One of the oldest monkeypod trees in Honolulu covers the entire front yard at Borthwick's home on Wyllie Street. A Moreton Bay fig *(ficus macrophylla)* about 125 years old grows in Queen Emma Square. It was planted in the old Royal Gardens established on this site by King Kamehameha IV.

We began to lose some of our older, now extraordinary, trees in the sixties. One of the trees on the American Forestry Association's "Social Register of Big Trees," a sandbox *(hura crepitans)* in Moanalua Gardens, was felled for a state highway interchange. A number of other large trees were lost at the same time, but one of the largest monkeypods in Honolulu still struggles for survival between steel protective railings in the median strip of the H-1 freeway. An earlier successful fight by Outdoor Circle supporter Alice Spalding Bowen saved the tremendous Indian banyan growing at 'Iolani Palace, but then a dozen of the mahogany trees on Kalakaua were cut to make a left-hand turning lane that was never used. The state tried the old carnival shell game on Dillingham Boulevard, trucking in coconut palms from Wai'anae and replanting them along the airport entrance road to appease the Outdoor Circle; then later the state uprooted the palms when construction commenced on the airport freeway and replanted them God knows where.

In the old days people were much more happier, I think. Now we have more people and more people are interested in making more money, money, than like the old style, very leisurely, less traffic, less people ... Now buildings unbelivable, unbelievable. Especially on Fort Street. Never expect these tall buildings compared to the low six stories. Old time Aloha Tower was the tallest building. Young Hotel wasn't too tall. Now the buildings are more twice the size ... I have one kid very happy in San Mateo. One is happy over here. The one here is more of a money-making man. All he does is try to make money, working very hard. But that's like Honolulu now.

Robert Lum
Retired Grayline driver

The yellow shower, one of many varieties of flowering trees that brighten every Honolulu street, drops most of its green leaves to produce a golden glow.

The city attempted to remove the rows of giant ironwoods along Kalakaua extension in Kapiʻolani Park, claiming they were full of termites and might fall down on tourists; but vociferous opposition stopped the chain saws. Traffic engineers, supported by the City Council and the mayor widened Keʻeaumoku and King Streets, removing a beautiful 100-year-old banyan with a canopy so large it extended clear across the intersection. Community opposition to destruction of the Keʻeaumoku Street banyan reached a climax on the Sunday morning scheduled for cutting, when I helped organize "memorial services" for the tree. Artists arranged for a "paint-in" and photographers took their last pictures. The mayor announced plans to perpetuate the now-famous tree by dismembering it and planting its limbs in various parks around the city. After the remains had been removed by city workers, someone placed a small white cross in the scarred earth, reminding the drivers on Keʻeaumoku that something old was missing from Honolulu.

Killing of the banyan caused a strong public reaction and undoubtedly led to the chain-sawing, very early one morning, of the graceful circle of royal palms that once surrounded King Kamehameha's monument in downtown Honolulu. The palms had been planted many years ago, with proper dedicatory services, in front of the Judiciary Building, one of Honolulu's most significant historical sites, and it was incredible that anyone would destroy them; but the local tree-trimming crew *luna* claimed the state ordered them removed. When pressed he said he had no copy of the work order, but the man who authorized him to cut down the palms said his name was Albert Camus.

While enraged state officials continued to denounce what they described as a meaningless prank pulled by a "screwball," a University professor thought he saw a meaningful message in the act. The choice of the name Albert Camus could be no coincidence when viewed against Honolulu's recent record of sacrificing historic and aged trees for highways and subdivisions.

Albert Camus stressed in his writings man's need to carry out a personal responsibility in the fight against social evil. Camus, a member of the French Resistance during World War II, wrote, "considered as artists, we perhaps have no need to interfere in the affairs of the world. But considered as men, yes . . . I have written so much and perhaps too much, only because I cannot keep from being drawn toward everyday life, toward those, whoever they may be, who are humiliated and debased. It seems to me impossible to endure that idea, nor can he who cannot endure it lie down to sleep in his tower." The royal palms were never replaced.

In 1925 the city authorities had tried their best to extend Hotel Street through the center of historical Thomas Square, a park opposite the Honolulu Academy of Arts, and were stopped by the state legislature, which at the urging of the Outdoor Circle, passed a resolution asking the city to cease and desist. Fifty years later the State followed up by passing Hawaii's Exceptional Tree Act in 1975. The same year Mayor Fasi appointed Honolulu's first County Arborist Advisory Committee. It's been a running battle to outwit the city and state, but we may yet win the war. ■

The young people of Hawaii do consider Honolulu as a gathering place. They like a bit of the big town atmosphere and yet like to relax away from downtown, and because of the good roads and cars they're willing to ride away from downtown and enjoy themselves 10 or 15 minutes away from downtown, but still in Honolulu. And the kids who are trying to make a living look forward to living on a neighbor island, perhaps, but still working in Honolulu because it is the gathering place. With new people coming in from the east, west and south, it makes it very much the crossroads of the Pacific we always talk about. It's a nice place to gather, and well, "do your thing," you might say. It shows so much diversity. Almost anything you want to do you can do in Honolulu.

William S. Richardson, Chief Justice
State of Hawaii

This is still one of the least expensive places to come to and one of the safest places to come to in the world.

J. Akuhead Pupule
KGMB early morning disc jockey

It is Aloha Friday in Honolulu and the island *muʻumuʻu*, in every color and design, decorates the city. Overleaf, urban Honolulu covers the land between the mountains and the sea. Diamond Head and Waikiki lie beyond.

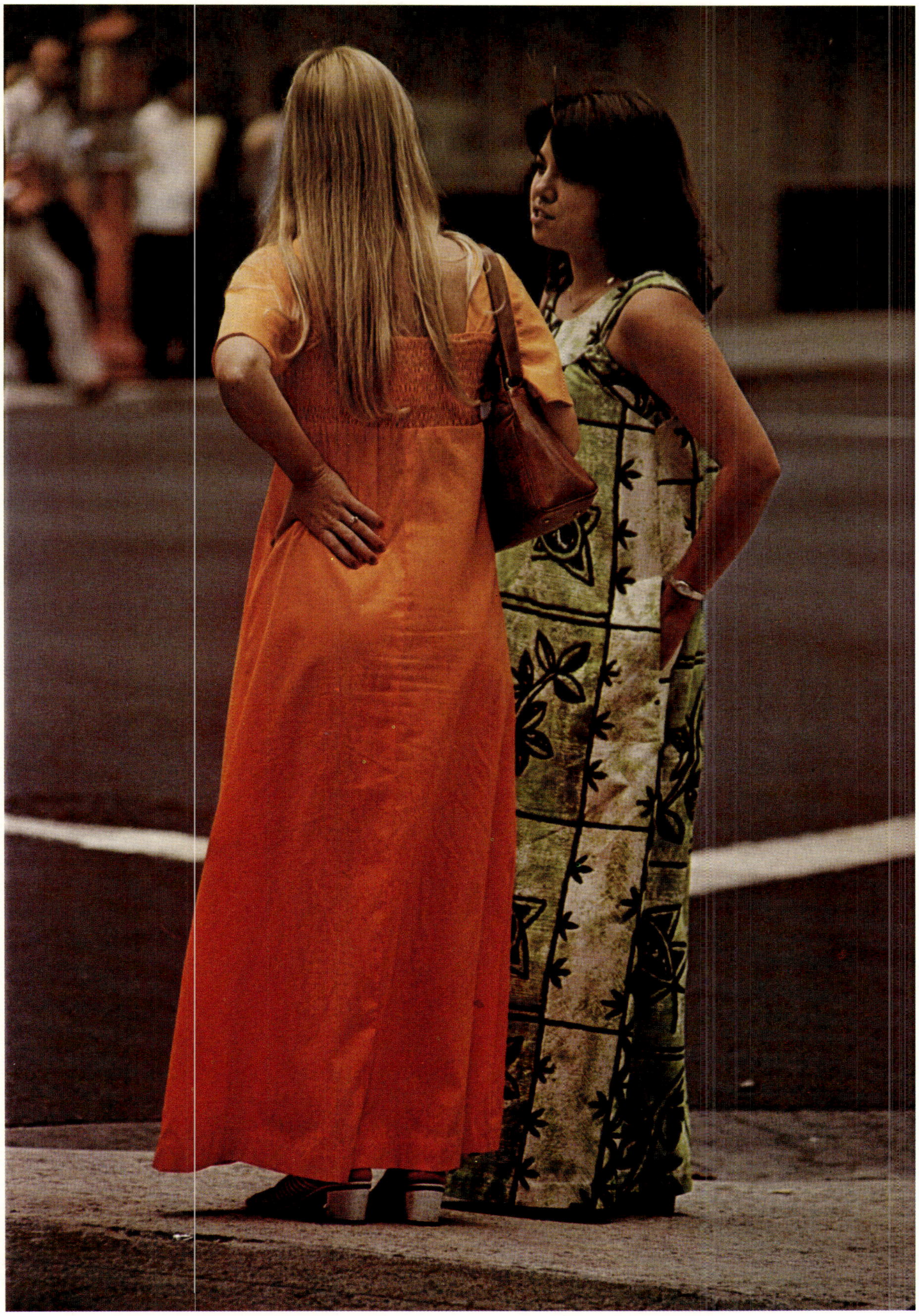

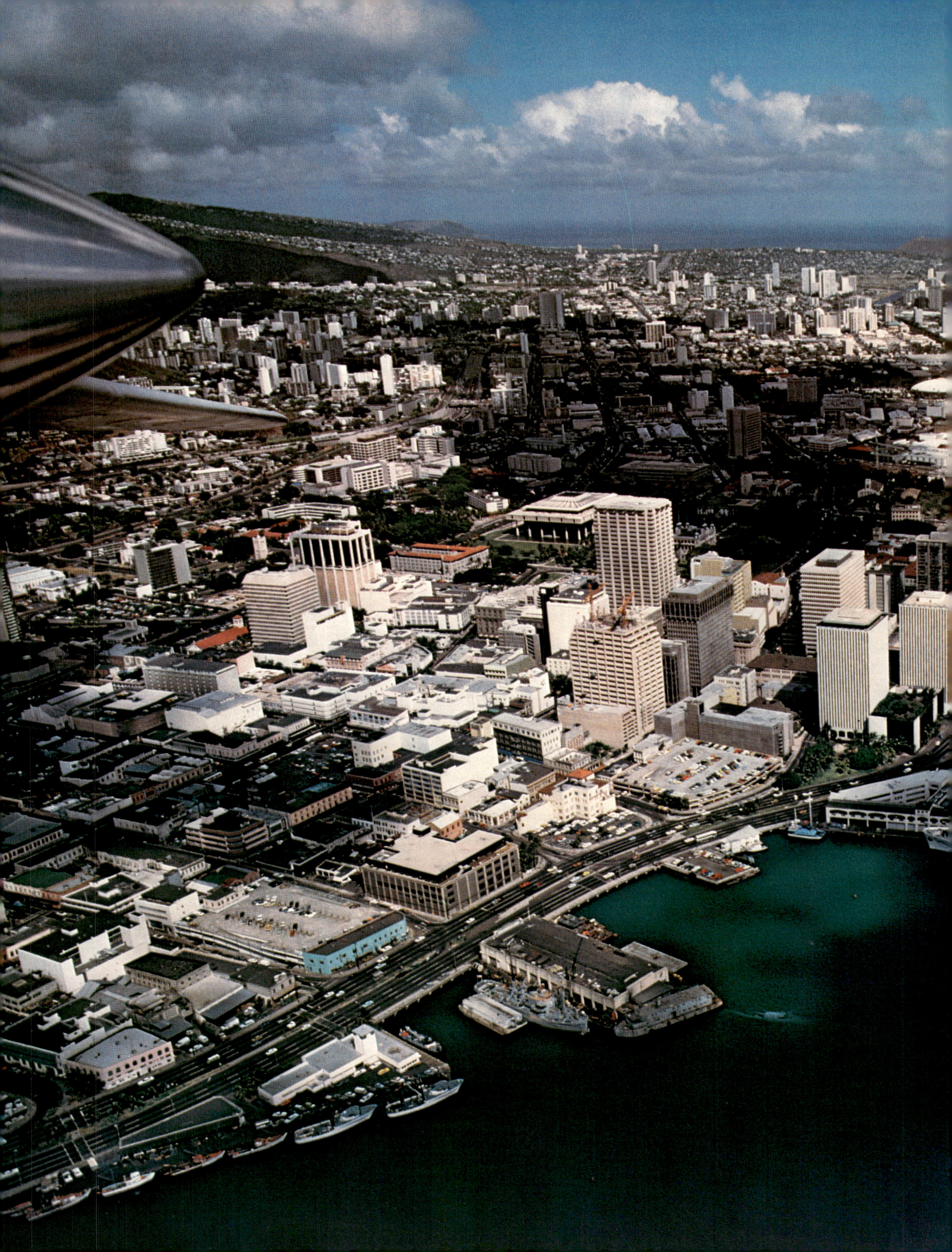

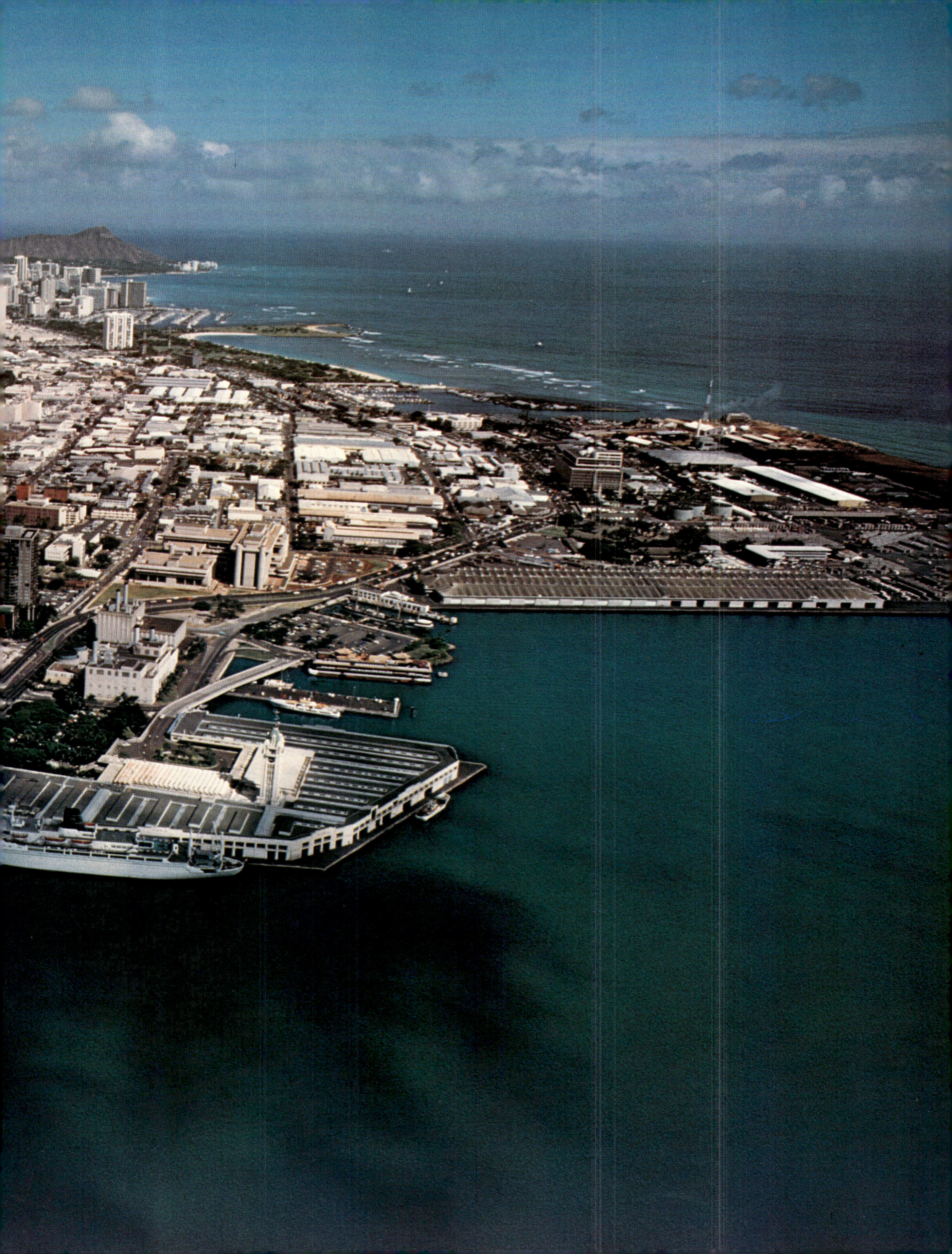

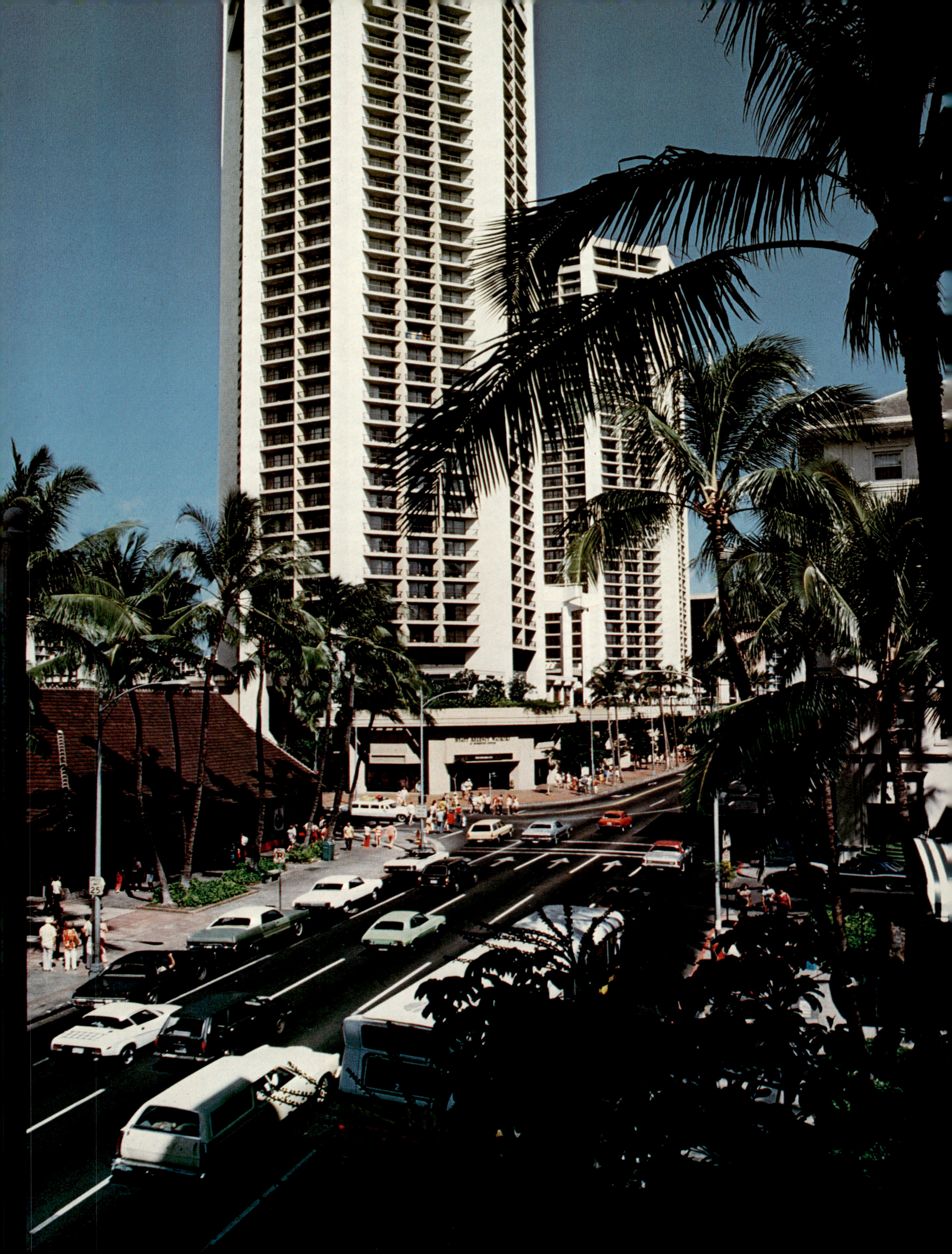

Kalakaua Boulevard Is Waikiki

Waikiki is one of the world's great walking places. Not along the narrow beach, for there is no Boardwalk like in Atlantic City, but along the sidewalks of Kalakaua Boulevard. It's Hawaii's version of the Ginza in Japan, of Michigan Avenue in Chicago, of Fifth Avenue in New York. Kalakaua is not the ritzy "seen and be seen" street of Rodeo Drive in Beverly Hills, nor is there the history and romance of Paris's Avenue des Champs-Elysêes; but to the visitor, Kalakaua has much of the excitement of all these streets contained within the two-mile central Waikiki core. It's slightly dingy, almost risque, and promises more than it delivers, but it's where "the action is," where something seems to be about to happen at any moment.

Kalakaua in Waikiki begins at Ft. DeRussy, where servicemen on leave from every branch of the military first blend with vacationing civilians and are drawn toward Diamond Head hidden somewhere behind the solid phalanx of hotels, condominiums, and office buildings. Slender coconut palms soften the concrete hulks facing each other across the wide boulevard that is never empty of traffic.

Kalakaua begins totally undistinguished and actually quite seedy, with garish islands of honky-tonk before it settles down into a consistent style and flavor. In the first block, discount gift shops, adult movies, and gift bazaars compete for customers and offer little evidence of anything worthy. Canlis and Chez Michel, two of Honolulu's best restaurants, squeeze in where each would be least expected.

One of Waikiki's two McDonald's is well-disguised within the elegant blue-tiled Gumps Building across from the likes of "The Pearl Factory," "Garment Factory to You," and the "World's Fastest Overnight Film Processing." Here is Woolworth in a bank and office building, and the "Deli–coffee Shop — Kosher Style" next to the new Waikiki Shopping Plaza. Hardly a distinguished collection of shops for any worthy street, but Kalakaua combines this frothy mix in just the right proportions to satisfy the insatiable street appetites of perhaps 70,000 tourists, night and day.

Kalakaua Boulevard, Waikiki, 1941.

I came to Waikiki alone one month ago. For me, each new day has been a miracle. I have welcomed each new dawn — in awe and humility . . . Regretfully and sadly I leave. I take with me beautiful memories and many intangible gifts from your people — Smiles, the touch of a hand and caring. Where else in the world does one see picnic benches carved with hearts and love instead of filth? Where else does one find a sidewalk full of soapsuds or windows being washed early in the morning? Where else can one learn the hula and quilt making only for the asking? Is this what the critics call commercialism? . . . I'm going home a richer, healthier, happier person because I have been to your enchanted haven of Honolulu — and I shall return.

Viola Ulberg, tourist
Helena, Montana

Kalakaua Boulevard, Waikiki, 1978.

There are also McDonald's in Hawaii — 28 of them, with the notable difference that in addition to green shakes and quarter-pounders, they serve up heaping plates of hot rice, oriental saimin, and spicy Portuguese sausage with eggs.

Bright splashes of *aloha* shirts and missionary-styled *mu'umu'u* covering everything from neck to toe invite casual shopping in window-front stores, which need to offer little in choice of stock when many of the first tourist purchases are matching shirt and *mu'umu'u* in the most garish designs imaginable. They are suitable for nowhere else on earth, but none is intended for back home.

Waikiki is the place where changes in identities and philosophies are subtle and sometimes irreversible, for here is the place of escape. Arriving from stuffy mainland cities in coats and ties, plain slacks and bouses, the hotel room is only a brief stop to strip away mainland encumbrances and step into the brand-new world of Hawaii. The warm, humid air of fabled Waikiki is absolute proof that paradise exists. A stroll down Kalakaua is a symbolic release of lifetime conventions and unsuspected inhibitions. For many, Kalakaua is a discovery of living, and the realization that with even a simple change of clothes almost anything is possible. The discovery of new people and a new self adds dimension and excitement to the Kalakaua scene, making the experience itself an encounter of a new kind.

Open shirts, string bikinis, and short shorts are street dress on Kalakaua. They mix comfortably with yellow city buses, red cycle rickshaws, and the steady stream of automobiles also sightseeing through Waikiki, dodging surfboards on bicycles and brown sunbathers with straw beach mats and airline flight bags. It's warm here, and next to nothing is the fashion from early morning until late night, with visitors walking from off-beach hotels to the ocean and from on-beach hotels across the street to stand in line for breakfast at Minute Chef or to wait for their round-the-island tour bus to arrive, coupons and camera at the ready. The buses creep around back streets searching out their hotel stops,

Changes in Honolulu over the years have been awesome, astounding. The superlatives never stop, particularly for those of us that date back a little while. As we look around, the profile of Diamond Head is harder and harder to single out. When I started there were about 5000 hotel rooms on the island of Oahu. Now we have approximately 30,000 rooms in high rise hotels all around us. Our hotel is the only one that has stayed the same like in the old days.

Honolulu is the cultural center. It's the center of finance, the center of fine arts . . . the island is large enough so that it encourages people to speculate in motion, movement, sightseeing. There is a great deal of life and vibrancy, a great deal of jubilation . . . It is difficult to envision something like this being duplicated on the neighbor islands. The neighbor islands have their own aura, and I think everyone agrees that you don't want to repeat many of the things that have happened in Waikiki. But, nevertheless, it is still the gathering place and for the foreseeable future there will be little that can deter the movement of people to Honolulu.

Randy Lee, Manager
Halekulani Hotel

traveling close behind each other like multicolored caterpillars. They park together, and travel together, picking up and disgorging loads of tourists together, as if afraid to be separated in the wilds of Waikiki.

At the Royal Hawaiian Hotel entrance, Kalakaua Boulevard straightens out and coconut palms shrink in size as high-rise hotels grow higher. Only a glimpse of Diamond Head's profile can be seen between hotel towers. They loom high — above the eyebrows at International Market Place, the only space still open to the sky along Kalakaua, before Kuhio Beach Park where the solid concrete wall is broken, permitting fresh ocean smells to blow across the street. A large banyan tree grows here, surrounded by unusual benches with roofs attached. The sign overhead says "Warning: Beware Bird Droppings." It's a favorite nesting place for mynah birds and local residents.

Across the street is Hyatt's Regency Hotel, built on the site where Peter Canlis invented the steak and lobster combination in 1947. The first Canlis restaurant was installed inside an old wood residence converted by Peter's architect friends, Pete Wimberly and Howard Cook, into the first steak and lobster house in the world. Postwar strollers on Kalakaua remember the great clouds of billowing spicy smoke produced by Peter's new charcoal broiler. It could be smelled on yachts a mile at sea. Thirty years ago there were only seven items on the menu, and lobster was $4.50. Today the Canlis restaurant at the other end of Waikiki has 30 items on the menu, and lobster is over $16.

Canlis has an astonishing employee record. The headwaitress, Kuni Kawachi, began working at the original Waikiki location in 1947. She and her sister, cocktail waitress Skoshi Uyemura, have worked for Canlis 31 years.

Tahiti's South Seas Spectacular rocks the Beachcomber Hotel's Bora Bora Room in Waikiki. Afficionados who have "watched the hands" in Waikiki hula shows over many years have noted that *ti* leaf hula shirt lengths go up and down with contemporary mainland fashion.

I think that growth on this island should come virtually to a stop ... I hope that growth here certainly from the tourism standpoint will come to an end pretty soon, particularly when they reach the limit of rooms in Waikiki ... One of the problems you face with government is it takes an awfully long time to get things done. The Governor's Travel Industry Congress of 1970 recommended a limit on the number of hotel and condo rooms, apartments, in the Waikiki area. It wasn't until 1976 that we finally got action by the City and County of Honolulu to actually put those limits into law. If I recall correctly it's about 26,000 hotel rooms and about 3000 apartments ... We're getting very close to that. Probably another year or so and it should see us at the limit. It's not going to hurt. People will not be refused the opportunity of coming here, because there's very simple things that happen in tourism. We've been experiencing this for a long time — the change in the length of stays. People used to stay here for weeks. Now, we've gotten to where the average length of stay is about ten days or so ... What can very easily happen if you have a limit on the number of rooms and the tour operator wants to send more people here, is to change his packages to decrease the length of stay in Waikiki and take them to the other islands for the rest of their Hawaii visit.

John Simpson, President
Hawaii Visitors Bureau

Japanese tourists may eat at Marushin, Americans at Canlis and at Bagwells. Tourists on a budget split hamburgers at McDonald's, and royalty dines in the Kahala Hilton's Maile Room. Eighteen different ethnic restaurants serve their national dishes in Waikiki, including Thai, Moroccan, and Greek. Eating out in Waikiki is indeed a tour of the world.

Kuhio Beach begins its crescent curve where Kalakaua bends seaward — still without revealing the famed profile of Diamond Head. Hundreds of surfboards are stacked in beachside lockers, near where pretty girls bake like lobsters in the tropical sun, white mainland skin barely hidden behind skimpy bikinis. Sailboats meander aimlessly on the horizon, beyond the gentle waves inshore where surfers rent a wave for a day.

Kalakaua gradually becomes seedy again opposite Kuhio, where "factory to you" outlets outnumber U-Drive car stands and whirling postcard racks. The silly pots of bougainvillea struggling to grow on lamp posts are discarded when Kapahula Avenue begins at Kapi'olani Park — where the full profile of Diamond Head is finally and suddenly spread across the sky. Kalakaua emerges from the tourist crowds of Waikiki and quickly transforms itself into a stately drive through the park.

Waikiki Beach is narrow and small compared to its reputation; but the first morning swim in its tepid, clear water and an outrigger canoe ride to shore on the crest of a wave that seems to last forever, evoke emotions that keep "sand in the toe," as locals put it. It's ocean spray in the face; a sky always clear; cool breezes on a hot, humid day; and shimmers of the setting sun reflecting across smooth waters inside the reef. It is the rainbows floating overhead on afternoon showers. It is drinking a mai-tai in the short twilight when day quickly becomes night and hotel *lu'au* torches are lit. No garish neon advertising signs gouge out the night sky; but never-ceasing traffic noise from Kalakaua is constant accompaniment for tin-can Tahitian drums in noisy Polynesian nightclub acts, and for more gentle Hawaiian melodies played on the guitar in contemporary slack-key. Joined together with the brass of dance bands and raucous rock, the sounds mix in a caterwauling tribute to Waikiki mania.

Nighttime entertainment mirrors the varied choices and contrasts of Waikiki, in local rescreenings of a late-late show arranged by tour packagers, and in commercially oriented nightclub operators catering to the music, dress, food, and living modes that are new here but old elsewhere. Hawaii has always adopted strange imports quickly, and the newest Hollywood aberration joins old flowers and people to augment further the Hawaiian mélange.

So, Honolulu and Kalakaua thrive, in a gently simmering *poi* bowl of island-flavored lifestyles stirred together with people, flowers, and cultures still arriving from overseas. No wonder the mainland visitors love the place. ■

I have an idea called Aina Malama — preservation of the land. I would like to see certain lands which are important to Hawaii's quality of life placed under the protection of the state Constitution — beyond the reach of the legislature, the Land Use Commission, county councils, and zoning boards. The people of the state should decide by vote which lands will be used for conservation, recreation, preservation of historical sites, and agriculture. Those lands should be placed in the Constitution and placed beyond the reach of those agencies. We will then have taken meaningful steps to protect those lands so that they can help maintain and sustain a quality of life for a long time to come.

I think I made a speech once where I said maybe the county government ought to be abolished. I have a feeling if we could sit down and have the neighborhoods come in — the people of the neighborhoods to effectively give input — we may be able to operate only with a state government. They get money from the county and state, and a lot of money from the federal government. Many of the services provided by the county can easily be assumed by the state. The county and city governments as we know them may not be necessary.

I do not think we should rest and be comfortable just because our crime rate is lower than some cities. I'm not going to compare Honolulu with others. I think what we have here now is not enough. Not good enough in terms of what we are and what we can become. Honolulu still has its attractions. It's better than New York. Better than Chicago. But so what? What is New York? It's failing. What is Chicago? It's not an example to look up to. It's like the people in the press and TV. Most of them here today are people from the mainland and that's the attitude they have. They think, well, this is better than New York or Chicago or Los Angeles, so it must be pretty good. But that's not good enough for me. I was born and raised here in Hawaii and I know what Hawaii was, and I want Hawaii to be what it can be.

Nelson K. Doi, Lt. Governor
State of Hawaii

Young Hawaiians at a Kapi'olani Park festival recapture their ancient Polynesian heritage while Waikiki at twilight (overleaf) reflects the excitement of a thriving resort on what was once a royal bathing beach. Only Diamond Head remains unchanged.

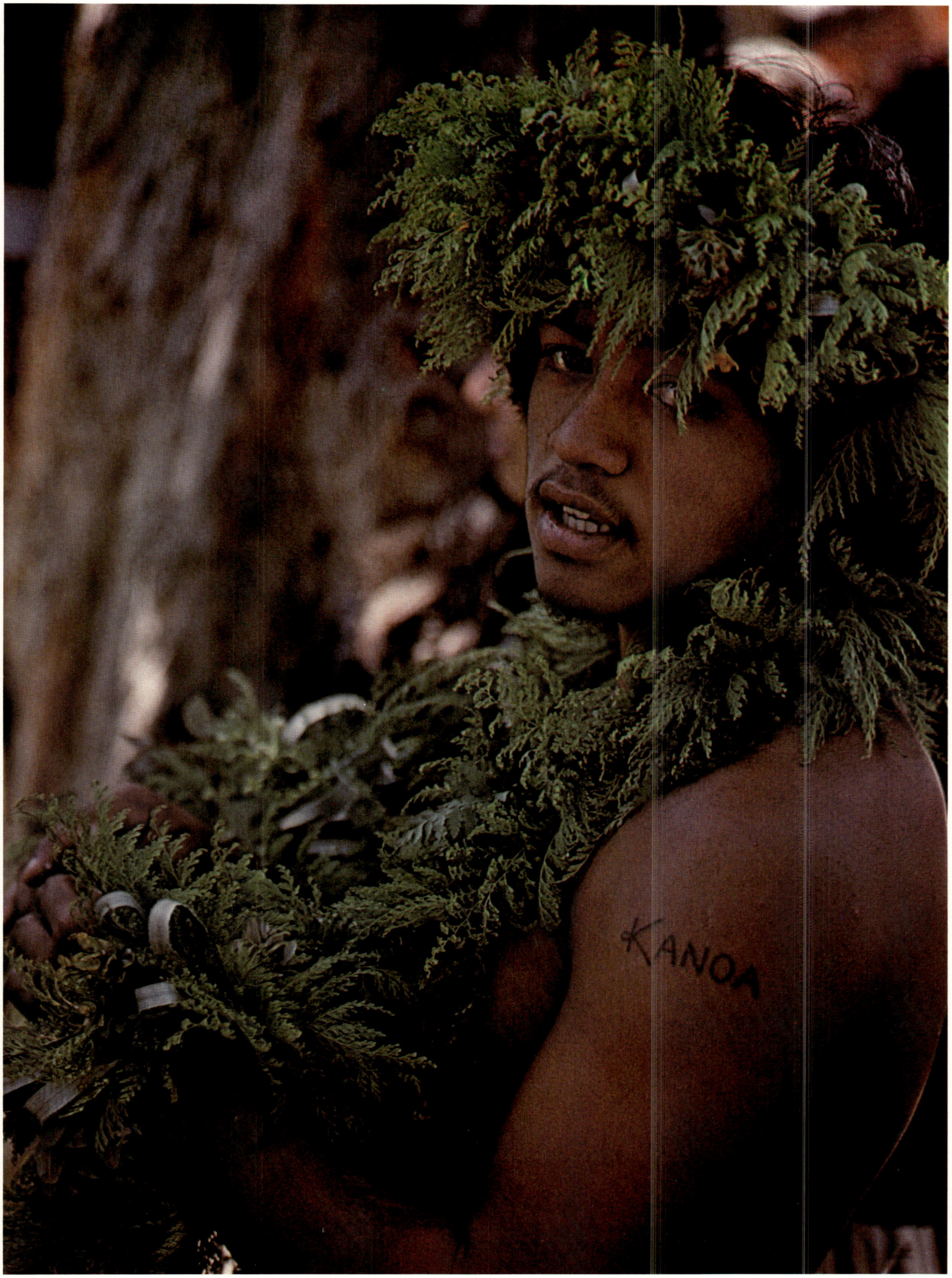
KANOA

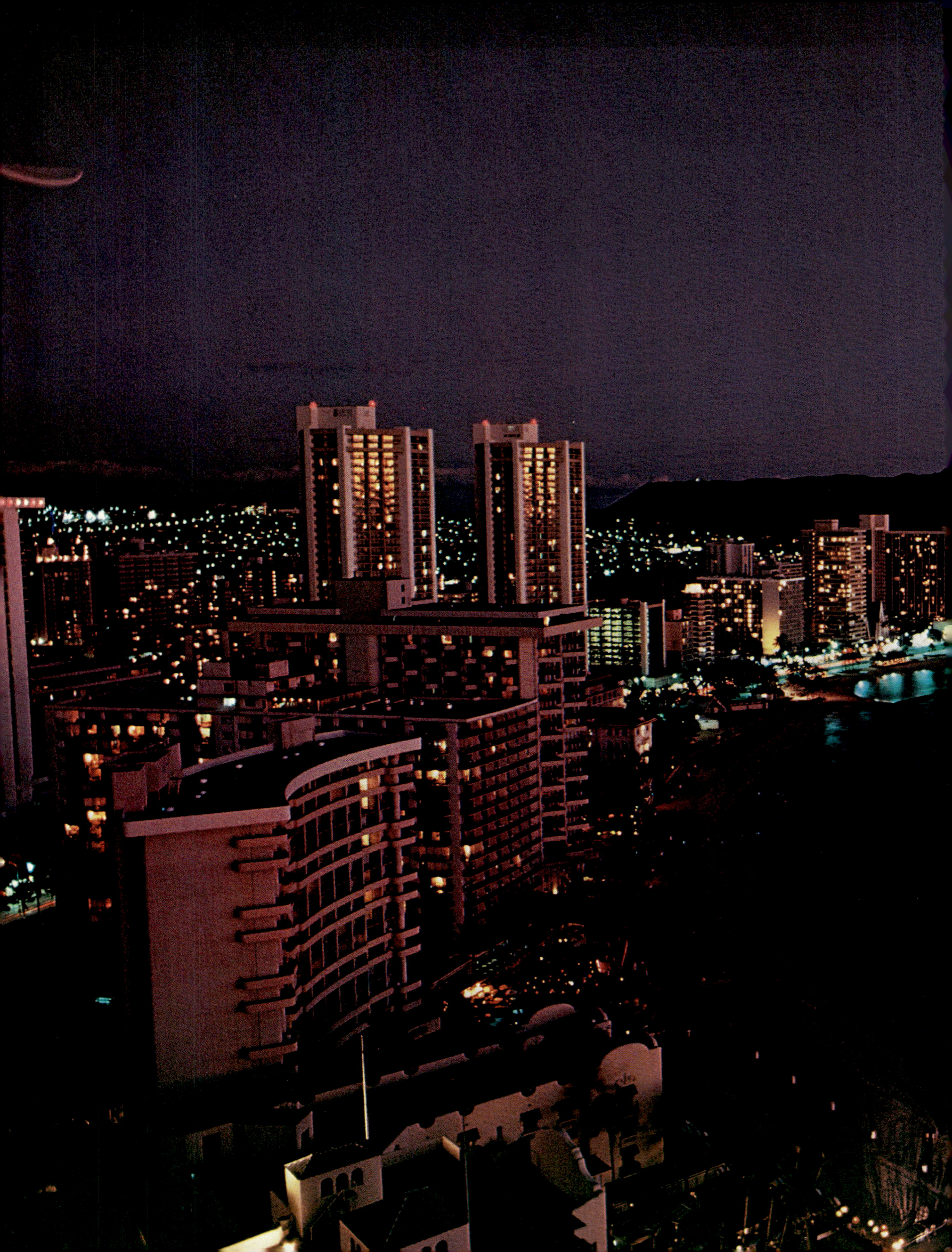

Certainly our growth is too fast and it needs to be slowed; but on the other hand, it's like plants. Either you grow or die. So, I would hope we continue to grow, but with a more planned pace and with a more sensitive attention to public facilities which are a necessary part of growth. . . . I hope that we can slow our growth to the point that we will not pass that divide which carries us from a small town to a metropolitan monster like New York, which has developed to the point where people are not received, judged, and communicated with quite as people. . . . This I hope Honolulu never comes to. It's one of my apprehensions of building a high-capacity transit system for Honolulu, because such a system stimulates growth because it's an attractive system to use, and growth around the stations can become just as dense as New York City or any other. And when you get that kind of thing, you lose the personal touch. Like when you stop speaking to people in elevators, then you're over the hill.

I love the mix of individuals. Not just in their ethnic background, but in their thinking. There is such a wide variety of approach to civic and business problems, and this is particularly stimulating. I came here from Charleston, South Carolina, and there the thinking is pretty much routine and there's not much difference between the groove and the rut. I like the individual thinking here and the differences of opinion on many issues.

Honolulu is still a small town and it thinks like a small town. The intimate acquaintance of people and their communications is still as it was when I remember it in the early fifties, and I think it's one of its beauties. The fastest way to get word around in this town is by word of mouth. . . . And as in many small towns, I think people seem to hear what they seek to hear according to their background. This happens here as well, and it still has that beautiful flavor of a small town, which I hope we never lose.

In the many times that I have to travel, particularly to the mainland, I squeeze that round trip ticket because I know that in returning to this Aloha Land I will be with people with whom I can communicate and with people who are worldly and understanding. I love them.

E. Alvey Wright, Former Director
State Department of Transportation

The *puka* through the *pali* was pushed through the Koʻolau Mountains in 1956, moving cars and people across the island to booming suburbs in Kailua and Kaneʻohe.

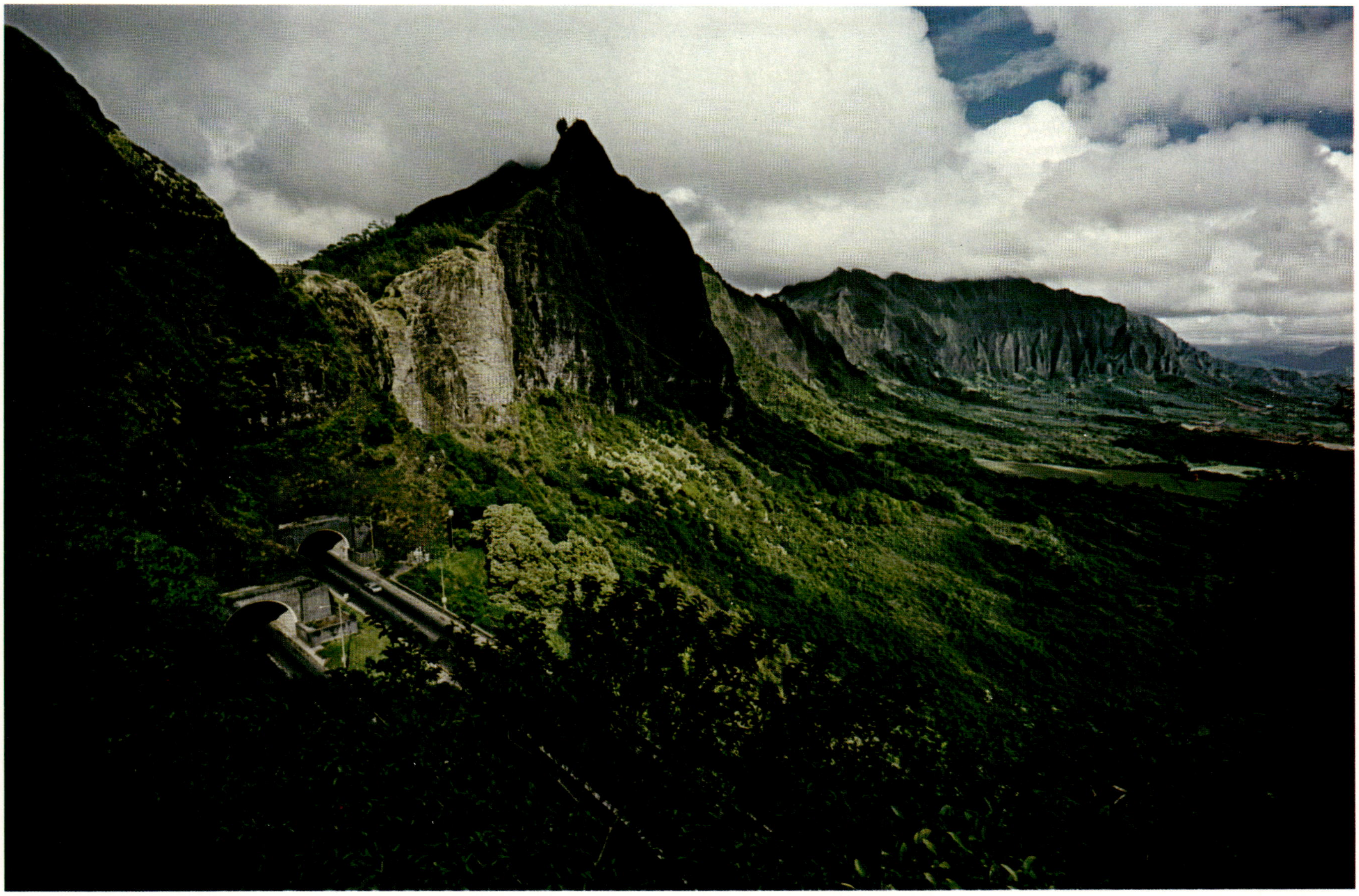

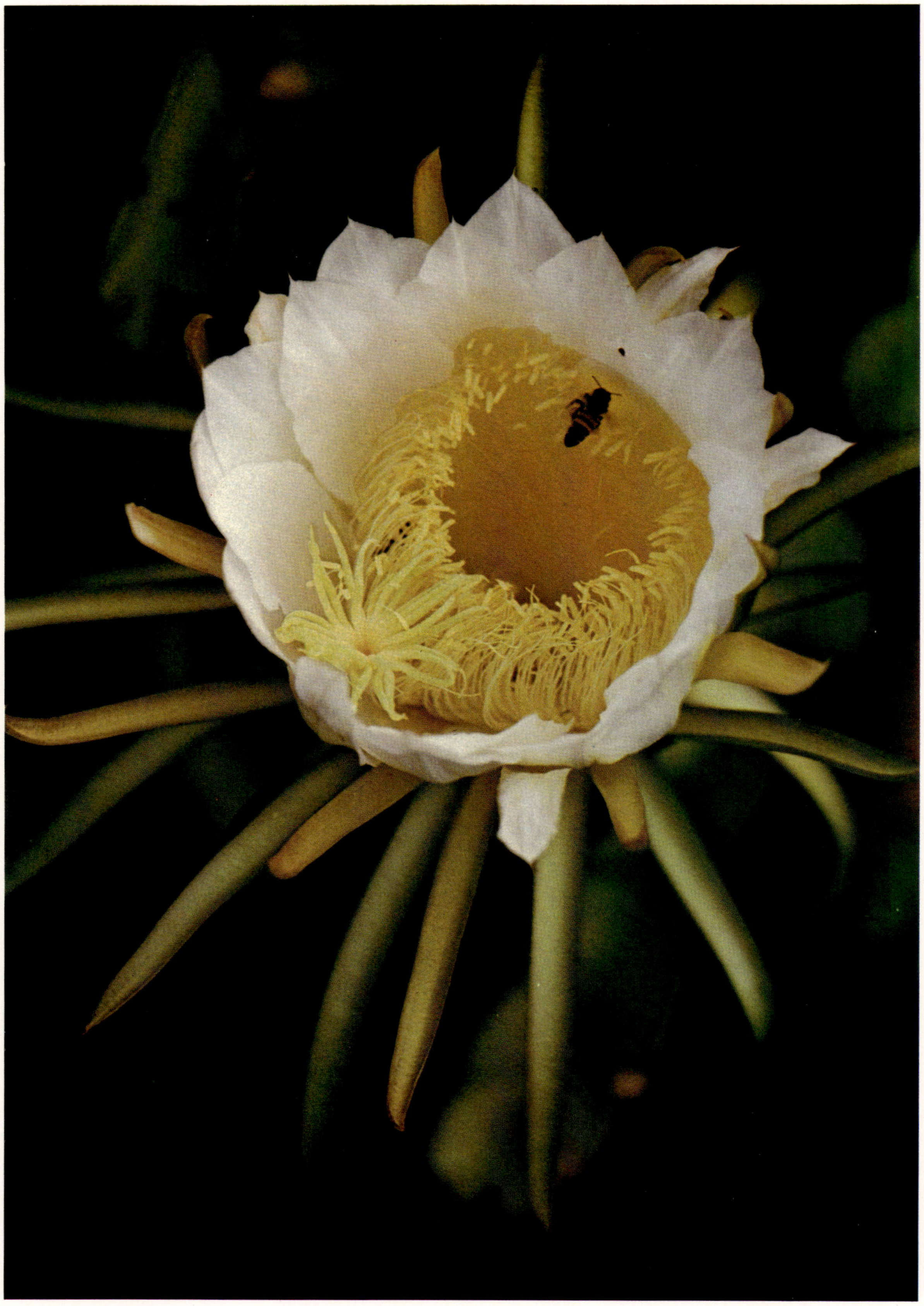

We Did It First

Oahu is a small island, but if you include the ocean around us it's a very big place, and living in Honolulu definitely extends beyond the shoreline (where we swim and sail), to the horizon (where we look) and above the clouds (where we fly). By this measure Honolulu is indeed a big place.

Honolulu is also a long place — the longest city in the world, measured from Makapu'u Point on the Molokai Channel to Kure Atoll at the northernmost boundary beyond Midway, about 1,400 miles and eight islands, depending on what size you call an island. The city charter includes all the leeward islands (except Midway), and this places all of Honolulu (except Oahu and Kure) in the Hawaiian Islands National Wildlife Refuge, an unusual distinction for any city, although some wags have suggested that Waikiki at times has sufficient wildlife to be included.

Honolulu has long been a collecting place as well as a gathering place. It has been a testing laboratory for new ideas brought in by travelers, who continue rediscovering Hawaii as if no one else had arrived before them — as if they were the first to learn of the island's unique lifestyle. And these "visitors" had always been missing the boat home (now they miss airliners and lose flight schedules), and many never do return where they came from. It is part of the local problem, an acquired affliction of *malihinis,* for the island environment seems to excite the dreamer, and we eagerly continue to hold out a *poi* bowl to stir innovative ideas and old traditions, for experiments with new visions. We have always been a place for original research in people relationships, which is rapidly leading to a completely new and original society.

And as the visitors came from different continents, so did the flowers, birds, and trees collected by early immigrants to live with them on their tropical landscape. The exotic botanical introductions thrived, as did the people, and soon most of the native living plants were crowded out and smothered by new arrivals, just as were the native Hawaiians. It was not possible to resist new introductions — the island plants and birds disappeared as rapidly as the Hawaiian culture and language. What remains is a dazzling botanical mosaic for the eyes, and a new societal treasure for the soul.

Imposed sometimes roughly upon this island foundation were economic and technological support systems also imported by pioneering merchants, traders, and planters intent upon transforming these isolated islands into a profitable enterprise. The island development occurred swiftly, with every problem, political and economic, quickly becoming a bold bridge to another goal.

Growers developed new varieties of sugarcane and pineapple to facilitate use of mechanical harvesting machines, to overcome disease, and to permit intensive use of herbicides and chemicals to control plant growth and sugar content. Eventually computers determined the optimum time to irrigate and fertilize, and when to harvest. Soon, the plantation manager just carried the message, making few decisions himself, and Hawaii continued to gain a reputation for getting things done better and more profitably.

Hawaii is a somnolent lifestyle gathered on a string of semitropical islands floating in just the right place. Not too far south in the Pacific, where humidity is a bother, nor too far north, where sweaters are needed, yet not too far west, where the wind blows hard. But Hawaii is far enough west to be that "different" place to visit and to do business where English is spoken, yet still a destination for escape from smog, city crime, snow, floods, hot summers, and cold winters. (With no seasons and ideal climate the Hawaiians had no word for weather.) It was only a matter of time before busi-

---

Honolulu is the smallest large city in which I've ever lived and it is the smallest in which I ever intend to live. I like the things that go with big cities — the cultural and business affairs, the transportation facilities to move internationally. Honolulu has it all, combined with the liveability of a small city. It's the only city its size in this country that has such easy access to everywhere. Honolulu is the international crossroads for the world's decision makers. Heads of state, advisors, cabinet members, principal military people, are easily accessible to us. It makes a very stimulating situation and one that is unique, I think, to Honolulu. It provides one of the elements for successful corporate leadership and is a characteristic which will help Honolulu as a future headquarters for international corporations.

James F. Gary, President
Pacific Resources, Inc.

Night-blooming cereus on the stone wall surrounding exclusive Punahou School, blooms for one night only. It is wilted and dead by first sunlight.

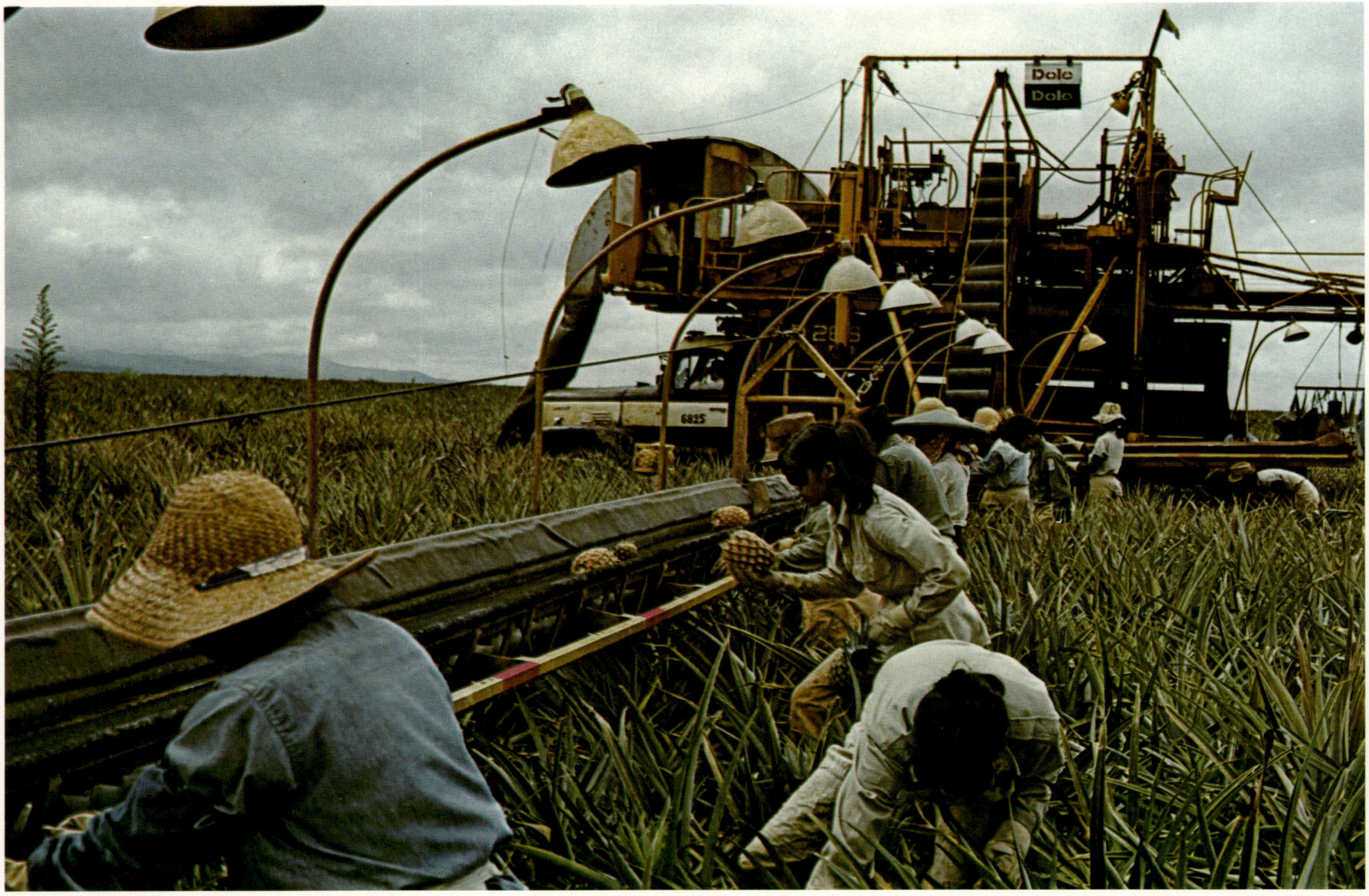
Dole
Dole
6825

nessmen and tourists found the islands and began to use them like home. In short order, local residents objected and, as rapidly as promoters and salesmen introduced mainland routine that changed the island way of doing things, residents responded with restrictive laws intended to keep the islands just the way they were. Some laws succeeded, some didn't, but in most cases Honolulu is still a beautiful island because we deliberately decided to keep it that way.

When the business visitors erected advertising billboards, the territory soon passed a law banning billboards (the first in the nation and still the only state law totally banning them). When new businessmen began using revolving signs and flashing neon to advertise their business, Honolulu became the first city of its size in the nation to prohibit all off-premise advertising signs and anything with words that shook, moved, or flashed. And in opposition to all principles of advertising display, laws require the sign must be small, so its message cannot be seen very far away! Electioneering politicians with squawking speakers were driven from the streets, and outside political display posters banned. Only bumper stickers, pedicabs and taxis remain as moving advertising space.

When it became evident all the island land was taken for one use or another — military, transportation, agriculture, urban buildings, hotels, or forest — and no existing use could be expanded without encroaching upon another, the state legislature decided in its wisdom to assume all zoning powers, and Hawaii's state land use law was enacted. With the counties being legal children of the state, it was quite proper to take away most of their zoning rights in the best long-range interests of all the citizens in the state. Hawaii was the first state to do so, and is still the only state with state-wide zoning. We were the first state to give farmers the right to dedicate their land exclusively to farming and pay lower taxes accordingly, even when their farms adjoined higher-taxed urban lands.

When too many hotels appeared on beachfront property, a shoreline protection law was enacted to keep them back. When excessive spear fishing began to deplete the once abundant sealife in Hanauma Bay, legislators created the first underwater marine preserve in the nation. When it was noticed that street improvements were in occasional conflict with trees, the first Exceptional Tree Act in the nation was drafted, giving the oldest, largest, and most beautiful trees equal rights with road builders. When office building and hotel owners protested high taxes on landscaped property, taxes were reduced to zero on gardens used by the public. And just to be sure nothing was overlooked, an environmental policy director with cabinet-level status was placed in the governor's office.

Honolulu cannot boast of a great "think tank" or a large industry to spur important inventions; but our isolation and relatively sudden thrust into the competitive business world has caused us to do much by ourselves, and to build major international corporate enterprises in the process.

Amfac's president, Henry Walker, is Honolulu born and his firm, selling under many different names, is one of the largest retailers in the West. Not only is it possible to stay in Amfac hotels on every main island in Hawaii, but also in Los Angeles, Las Vegas, on the rim of the Grand Canyon, and in Death Valley. Castle & Cook, with headquarters a block away from Amfac in downtown Honolulu, is the nation's fifth largest food processor, growing pineapple in the Philippines, bananas in Central America, sugar in Hawaii, and canning tuna in Oregon. Dillingham Corporation, whose founder built Oahu Railway, the first railroad in Hawaii, digs coal in Canada, barged most of the oil pipeline supplies to Alaska, and sells liquified gas in almost every state of the Union. Pacific Resources

---

Honolulu is going to be a bright star in the future of our country and the Pacific, where all the action is going to be, where two out of every three people in the world live in countries abutting Pacific-Asian waters. I think Honolulu has a destiny and the people living in Honolulu are beginning to realize how important Honolulu is to world peace, to our country and to the friends and neighbors who live in the Pacific-Asian area.

Frank Fasi, Mayor
Honolulu

Elaborate harvesting machines mechanize pineapple picking on the world's largest pineapple plantations surrounding Wahiawa. On the other side of the island, 30 minutes from downtown Honolulu, the lava rock shore and coral sand beaches extend to the horizon from Makapu'u (overleaf).

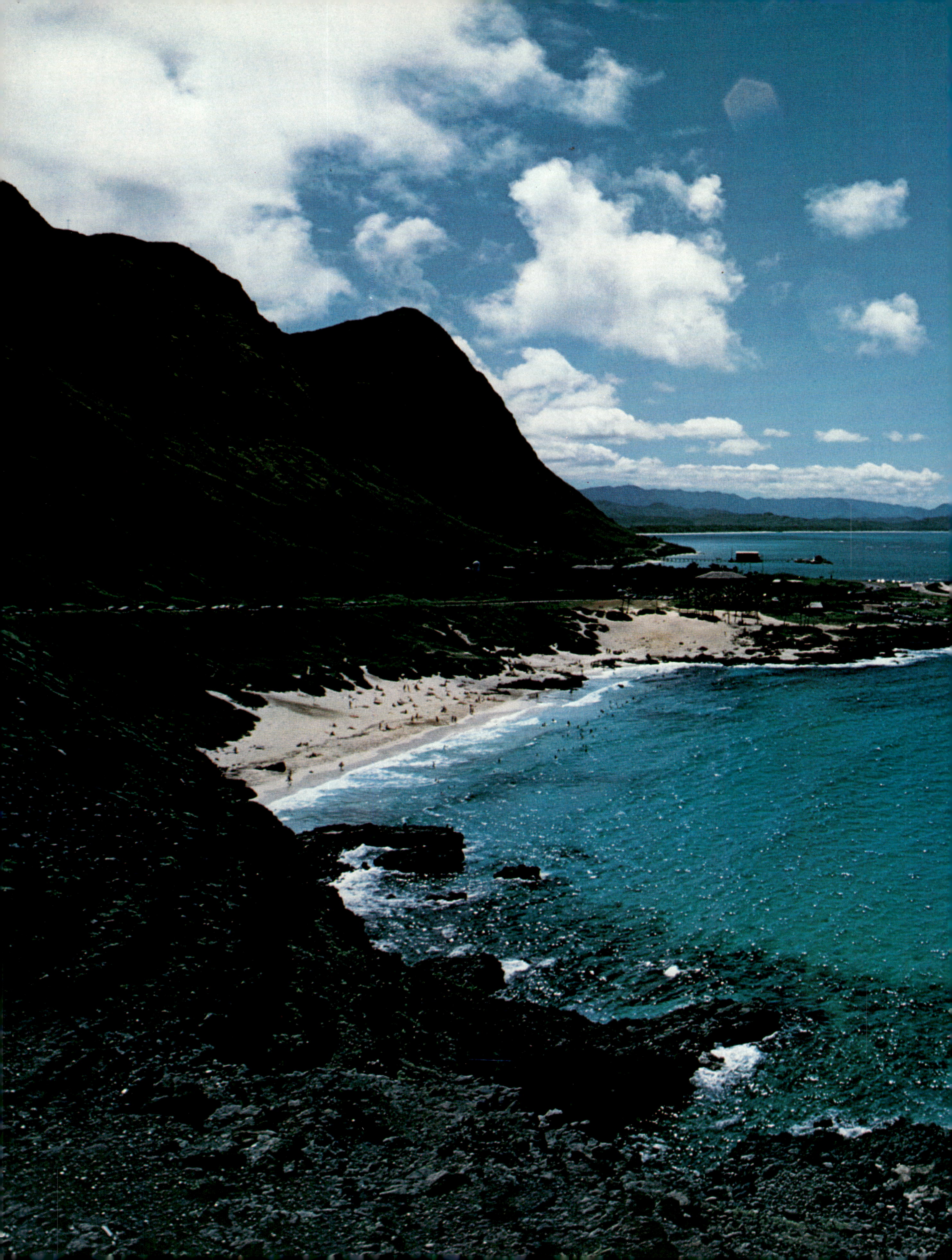

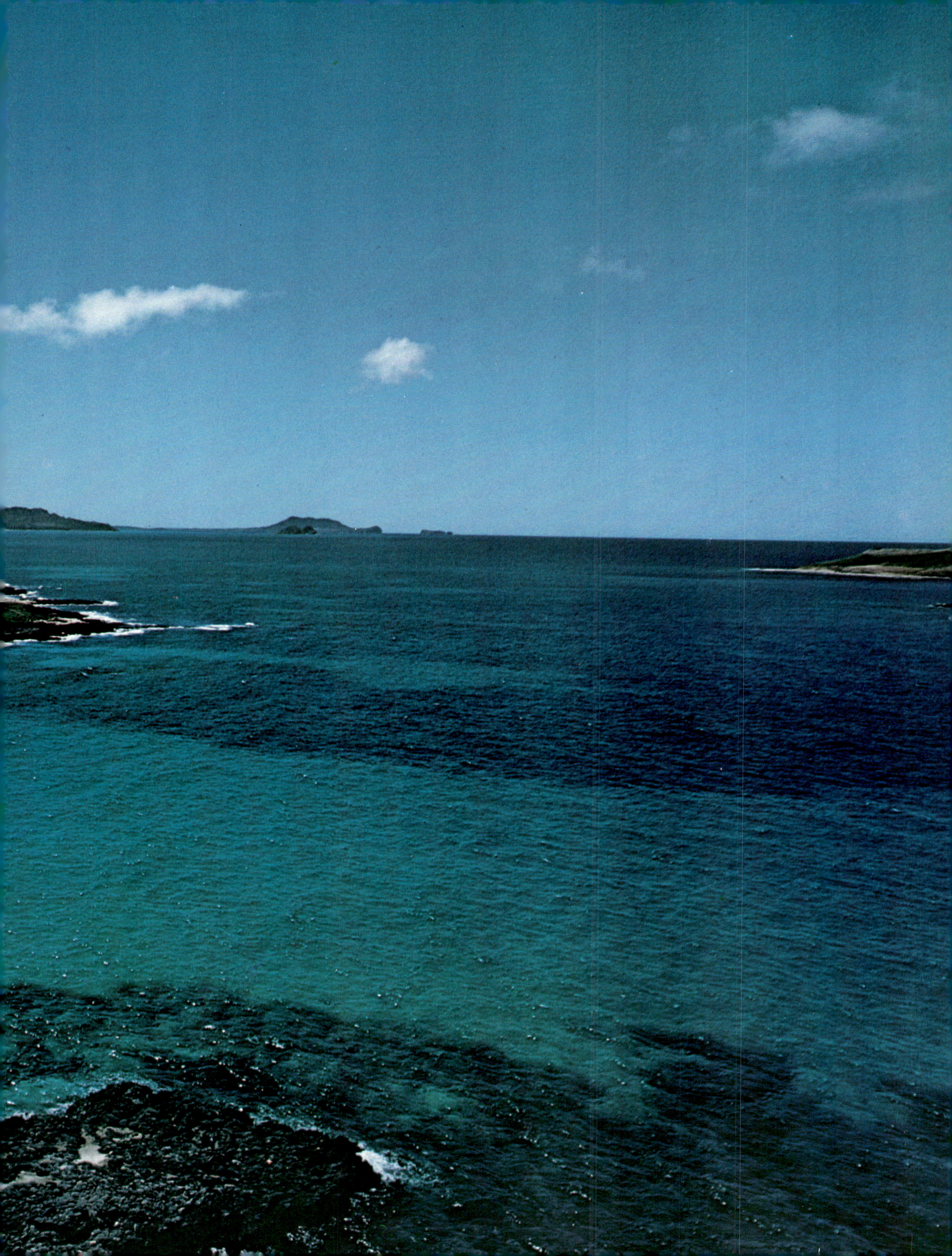

Flower *leis* of plumeria, orchids, carnations, and what is available that morning are strung for *kama'ainas* and tourists at airport *lei* stands.

operates oil tankers on every ocean and ranks number one in the nation in average sales growth over the past five years, a performance attributed mostly to an unusual activity for a Honolulu corporation — refining oil.

As a result of this business growth, Honolulu has many "firsts" to boast of, some not very important, but all ample evidence of our vitality as an island city. We used the first city-wide dial telephone system; we built the first revolving restaurant (Le Ronde, atop Dillingham's Ala Moana Building); we invented the condominium apartment, both vertical and horizontal regimes (the first one built under Hawaii's original law is at 3019 Kalakaua); we were first to establish legal limitations on the number of hotel rooms that can be built in a resort (about 29,000 for Waikiki, where there are now 23,000 rooms); and we had the first bottomless male waiters in the U.S. (at the Dunes Restaurant).

The first domestic scheduled hydrofoil passenger service started in Honolulu (Sea Flite), as did the first scheduled air cargo service (Hawaiian Airlines holds CAB Certificate No. 1). The two local airlines flying out of Honolulu (Aloha and Hawaiian) are the only scheduled airlines in America that have not had a fatal accident. Henry Kaiser built the first aluminum geodesic dome at his Hawaiian Village Hotel; we have the first movable bleacher sports stadium, convertible from baseball to football at the flick of a switch; and we enjoyed the first radio broadcasts west of the Rockies. Honolulu International was the first U.S. airport to service a commercial jet airliner (BOAC's De Haviland Comet III) on its first flight around the world.

Honolulu is a small kind of place where things vibrate more individually. It's also a small town where problems are temporary obstacles still solved by friendly cooperation. Even the usual governmental bureaucracy is easier to overcome when 82 percent of the state lives in one city, and when city hall is across the street from the capitol. It all fits neatly into Honolulu's sunny day, where the means to an end have always been the beginning. ■

Continuing to rely on tourism as the state's most important industry can be a self-fulfilling prophesy, as little effort will be made to diversify the economy. We could be looking into more light manufacturing, making more of the things we consume here. We can become exporters of energy, and self-sufficient in our foodstuffs, but all we are offered is more tourists. Must we become a vast collection of servants? Can't we be more like normal communities, engaging in a wide variety of healthy enterprises, supplying our needs with local manufacturing talent?

Dennis Callan
Life of the Land

Honolulu International Airport is a flying crossroads of the Pacific for 15 domestic and foreign airlines.

Everybody's Beautiful

Hawaii's Chinese (damn *pakes*) are all wealthy and spend 20 hours a day scheming how to get richer.

Hawaii's Japanese (damn budda-heads) are too big for their britches and spend 24 hours a day trying to control the state legislature.

Hawaii's Filipinos (damn flips) are pushy, dress in funny colors, and are getting rich on fighting cocks.

Hawaii's English and Scots (damn *haoles*) are arrogant no-goods who think they're better than everyone else and own everything.

Hawaii's Hawaiians (damn *kanakas*) don't like to work and are trying to take back their islands.

The stereotypes are everywhere — perpetuated by best-selling authors, and repeated without qualification by travel writers producing superficial froth simmering endlessly in racial melting pots. But the facts are simple. We found out long ago that what makes the living great in Hawaii is the differences, and nobody was a minority long enough to give anybody real trouble. Honolulu may be the only community anywhere with state funds being used to sponsor ethnic festivals like Chinese New Year and Japanese Cherry Blossom Week. We still have a separate Chinese and Japanese Chamber of Commerce, and another one where they speak English. It is the style of Hawaii to perpetuate the differences while we enjoy the differences. With keen competition for limited jobs and exploitation of favored positions in the economic and political communities, some rough edges will undoubtedly be ruffled; and if the street kids don't start a rumble on occasion, unrelated frayed tempers will. But long before the federal civil rights act, we had abolished our segregated "English Standard" school system and began living together on both sides of the street. There are no ethnic neighborhoods in Honolulu — everybody is all mixed up.

Of course, it all began with the Hawaiians, who had a very loose immigration policy — they let anybody in. When Captain Cook arrived, the anxious Hawaiian girls greeted his crew in their own flamboyant style and the mixed Hawaiian race was born. The missionaries (somewhat reluctantly), whalers, and proper merchants carried on the old traditions, giving birth to the Aloha Spirit, the neo-Hawaiian race, and the concept that everyone is beautiful.

Despite colonial attitudes of early businessmen who organized the great sugar factories, many did marry Hawaiian women — both commoners and members of royal families. Their descendents became social and economic arbiters of the islands and, in the case of merchant wives like Princess Bernice Pauahi Bishop, founder of the Bishop Estate, they had a continuing influence over the economic life of Honolulu.

The pattern was set long before Chinese and Japanese arrived to work sugar and pineapple plantations, with hopes of arranging for "picture brides" to be sent from home. For many sugar workers it was more convenient to marry the "native girl" at hand. It may be that the apparent acceptability of interracial marriages in Hawaii, and the children born of them, is partly because men have always outnumbered women in the islands. It was plantation policy to only contract for single men, and for many men far from home with little prospect of returning, marrying a part-Hawaiian girl was not only practical, but desirable. They were very beautiful women.

The Portuguese in turn made their cultural and physical contribution to the islands — soon there were Hawaiian-American-Chinese-Portuguese people. Portuguese immigrants also brought with them hot *malasada* doughnuts and *pao duce* to eat and the ukelele and guitar, both instruments adding considerably to the pleasure of

---

I went to the English-Standard School. It wasn't fair — wasn't fair. Haoles all went to the English-Standard, but there was a few taken — like a few Hawaiian and I was part-Hawaiian. They did give you a little test before you entered. I recall it very clearly, well, they showed you an apple and an orange. They wanted to hear you say the words. I looked quite Hawaiian and my German grandmother went with me. I can remember that, and they wouldn't dare to turn her down. So, there I was. But I spoke proper English, so there wasn't really any problem, but I suspect that others with no one to talk with them — one look and — so, sorry. We did have a few Chinese, but mostly a haole school. See, we were not very conscious of all that. In fact, we weren't conscious at all until we got quite a bit older. I don't think it was very necessary to separate the races, because even if I had gone to the so-called local school which was Kawananakoa I don't think I would have changed. The kids who went there didn't really speak the proper English, but how were they ever going to learn if they weren't associated with the kids who did speak properly?

Emilie Lemke Williams
Honolulu

Kahana Bay State Park.

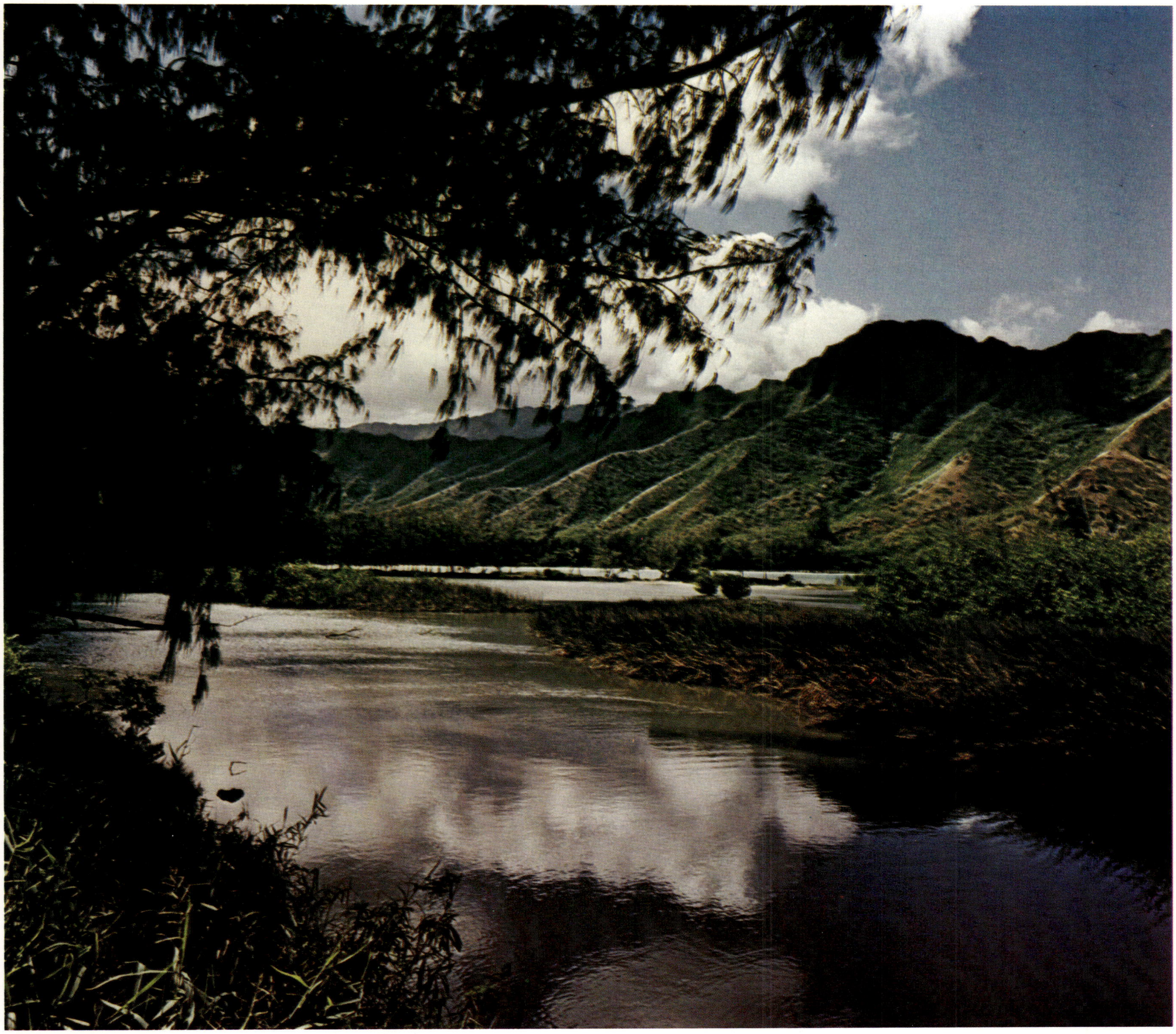

How is the fishing out here in Haleiwa?
It was good at one time, but not anymore because of population. Too much netting, diving. I believe for my type of fishing divers have destroyed most of the holes. I prefer line fishing with a boat. Go out — bottom fishing.
What for?
Used to be menpachi, but there's no menpachi now, so you have to go a little deeper for opakapaka, uku, ulua.
When do you go fishing?
Night is the best. That's for mostly akule and opelu. That's the main type of fish that we go for. It's the akule and opelu. We market right here.
What kind of price does fish get?
Oh, akule and opelu hasn't gone up in the last 15 years, but your exotic fish, y'know, the red ones, they've gone up — tripled. Like red snapper.
You're living kind of a retired life now?
Yeah. I just fish when I want to and I don't care too much for the commercial fishing. It's mostly for table use — family use. That way I don't have to spend a lot for groceries anyway.
Do you ever go crabbing?
We used to go. We used to get good Kona crab out here, but the law is too weak on crabbing. Now, they close crabbing for the summer, but it doesn't help.
What's the biggest fish you ever caught?
That's a marlin, 208 pounds. I marketed it. Marlin makes good smoke fish. Marlin is good for everything, steaks.
What kind of fish do you prefer?
For small fish, opelu. For sashimi fish, uku.
Are you always going to live here?
Downtown Honolulu is all business. Waikiki is all entertainment. The rest of the island is all mixed up with sugar and pineapple. It's more relaxing and I like it that way . . . Sugar out here is going to fade out eventually, because the zonings don't hold up. They're always changing it, so there's going to be more buildings. My home and lot is in a park zone. It was made park zone about ten years ago — can't even build a new home, can't do anything here. For a small man like me I can't do nothing.
Living is changing in the country then?
In the old days in Haleiwa we knew each other, knew everyone. We had no problem. We had no thefts. We had doors open day and night — closed, maybe, but unlocked. We had no trouble 'til a few years back. Then we started getting newcomers around. Things happened. You can't live around here now without a dog. It's not locals, it's all the newcomers.
Do you go downtown much?
I hardly go downtown unless I gotta go see a specialist. I never go for shows or parties or restaurants. I rather stay out here in the country. My life is full enough out here. Full of relaxation. Right? Relax with my beer. I hope life continues this way without too much encroachment by high rises or residential areas . . . You feel very tight downtown, and, well, you drive more carefully in town. We're not used to that type of traffic. Well, I guess maybe we wait too long to make a turn. There's more courtesy in the country than in downtown Honolulu. When you come home you just relaxed. The first thing you go for is a bottle of beer. When you come out of Wahiawa and down the hill you in third base, then almost home.

George Niimi
Fisherman, Haleiwa

Hale'iwa town on the north shore.

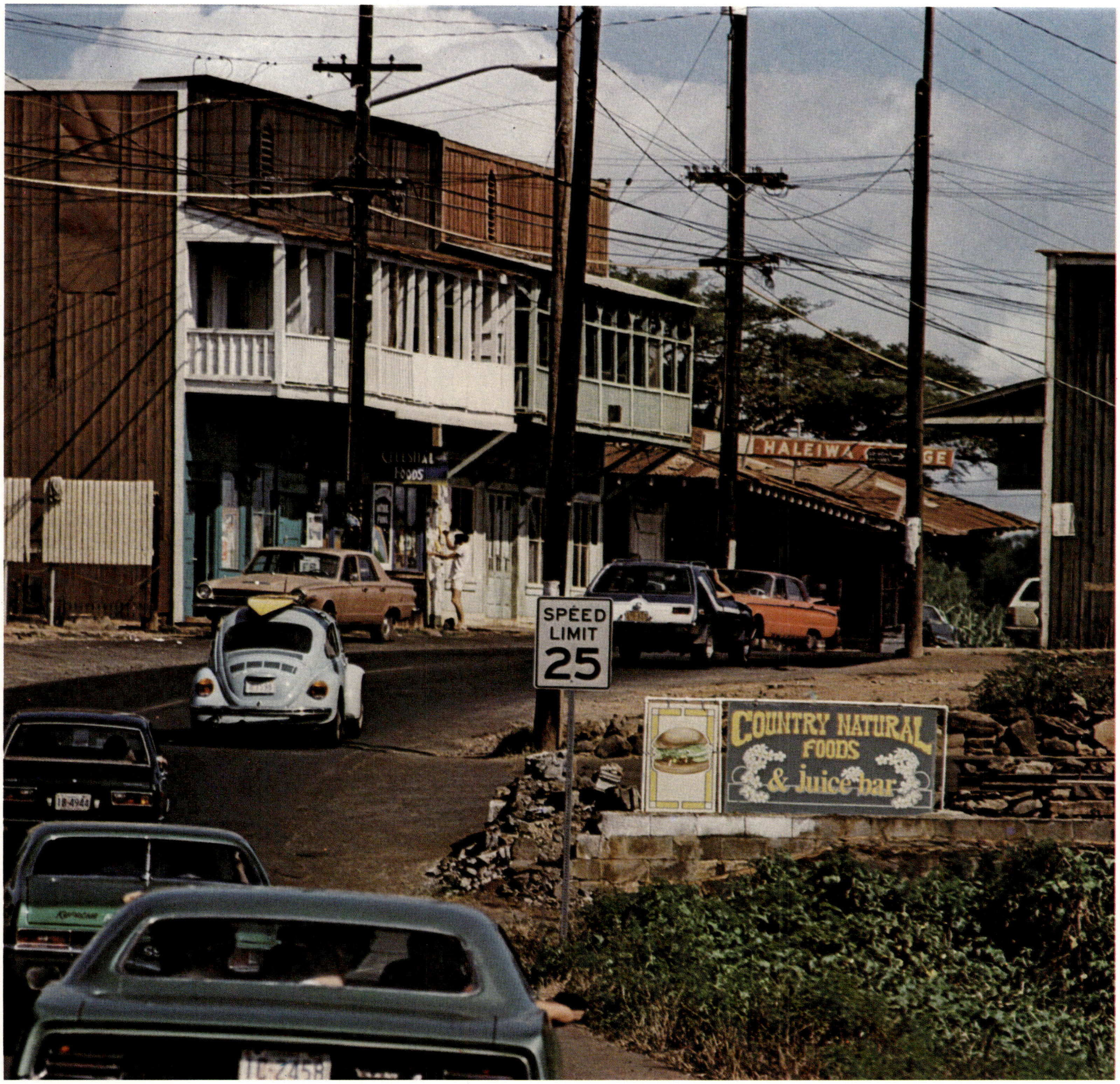
SPEED LIMIT 25
COUNTRY NATURAL FOODS & Juice bar

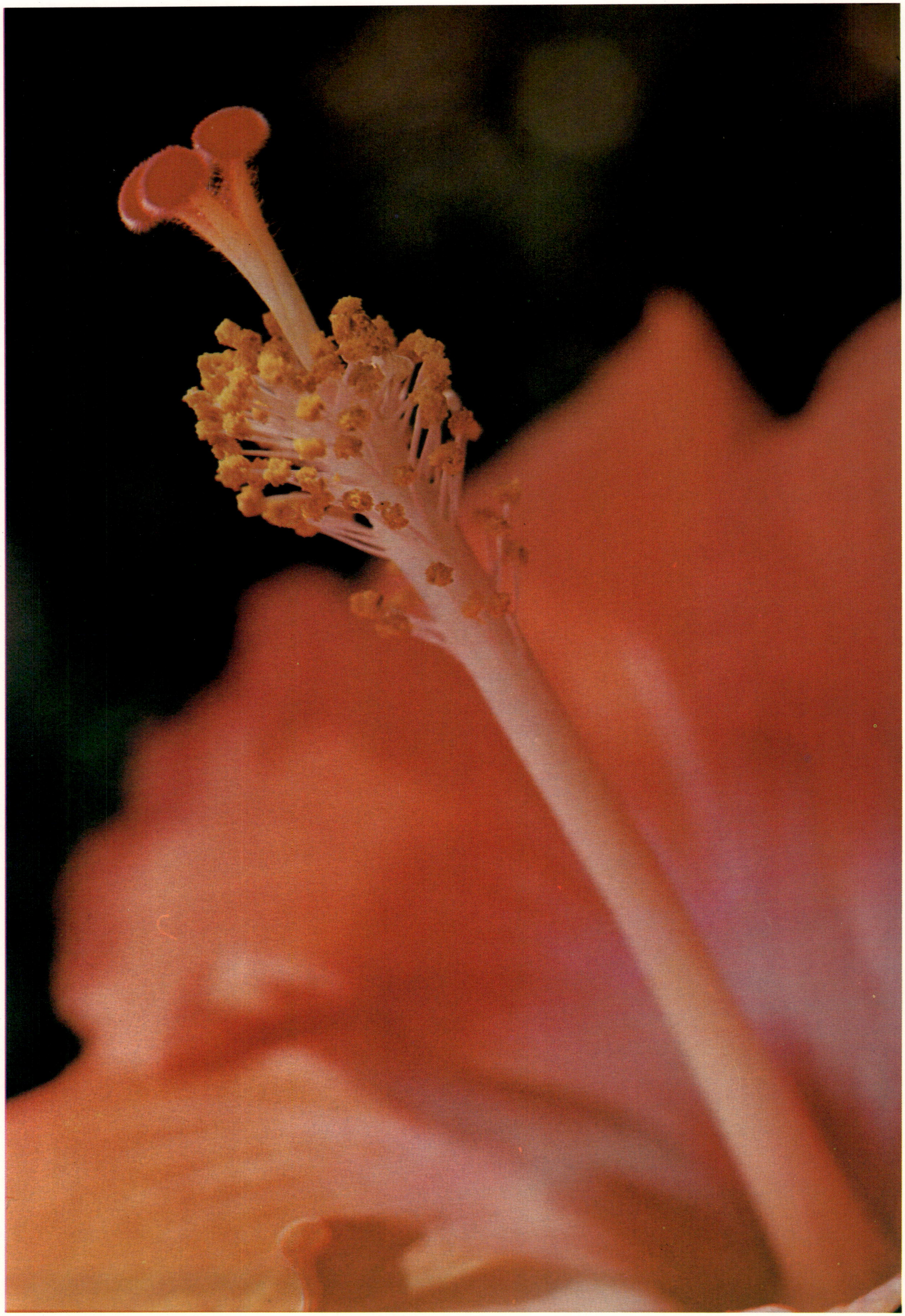

Hawaiian music. *Kama'ainas* still will joke about the Portuguese having been made *haoles* by act of the legislature, to make racial statistics look better to Southern congressmen in the struggle for statehood. Keeping racial statistics has always been a problem in Hawaii, where nothing matches up with mainland bureaucratic definitions, and where many interracial couples refuse to refer to themselves or their children as anything but American.

The final plantation immigrants were Filipinos, who are still barely represented in politics and business. Their numbers increase as new arrivals report home favorably on the democratic political weather.

Latest to arrive in large numbers among Pacific ethnic groups are Samoans, very much aware of their status as lowest on the totem pole in Hawaii's intricately woven tapestry of people. Still somewhat culturally isolated by age-old family relationships brought intact from their home islands, they have yet to join the mainstream of island life, and their cultural contributions are still to be felt.

In some ways, prejudice, or lack of it, can be measured by the degree that members of one group can enjoy a joke told on them by another. Like the story of the Portuguese who was raging about "damn *kanakas*," and after listing in great detail all the outrages committed by this particular Hawaiian, added, "And I tell you one ting! Dat damn *kanaka* — he sure can play one ukulele!"

What fighting there is in Hawaii may be mostly a family fight or the usual differences between the "haves" and "have-nots." Perhaps those who arrive in Honolulu with a chip on their shoulder, or who dislike the differences, would be better off in some state where everyone is alike. Hawaii's feelings may have been expressed quite aptly in a newspaper advertisement the day statehood was granted. The headline read: "Statehood For Hawaii — We're all haoles now."

Hawaii's epic story has too often been retold by magazine apologists emulating waves on the shore. Like the ocean surf they sweep words onto the beach and cover every disturbance in the sand. The waves quickly recede into the sea, smoothing out any irregularities remaining — erasing every trace of past events. They have glossed over the most exciting and controversial aspects of Hawaii's historical past, lessening the importance of our contributions to society by concealing the fact that we did trip and fall while growing up to statehood. Hawaii's renowned diversity and harmony, reluctantly resolved over the years, was born of severe economic and social struggle by immigrants from East and West who had no idea they were creating a completely new and original society, a cosmopolitan gathering place famed for its racial harmony. By the beauty of our differences and of our pride in shared responsibilities, we may well serve as an example to the world. After all, we did it ourselves.

What most of the rest of the world strives for is, in a real sense, what Hawaii already is. It is important to understand, however, that we did fight for the changes that removed Hawaii from yesterday — from cruel racism and alien worker exploitation. They were all shameful facts of a colonial outpost annexed by U.S. businessmen intent upon carrying out the biblical precept — multiply and subdue the earth.

The immigrants from Asia, North America, and Europe planted crops, built homes, started businesses, and imposed their special political and economic ideologies upon the islands. In the process they pushed the native Hawaiians aside, took their lands, and overthrew their kingdom. They corrupted Hawaiian dances and music. The soft Hawaiian language that missionaries had created in written form was virtually abandoned. In the process of joining a prosperous society, the Hawaiians lost everything — their land, language, and culture. Yet, in a way, they are still part of everything, racially and culturally, for every aspect of daily living in the islands reveals how much we owe our Hawaiian heritage. ■

I've been here since January, 1971, when I came from the Philippines. I was supposed to go to New York and try my luck there, but I happened to stop over in Honolulu because I have relatives here and I fell in love with the place and I stayed here. I felt at home here.

A lot of Filipinos move here and stay for good, because over here in Hawaii you have a chance to go up as long as you're industrious. As long as you work hard you can go on top.

Lettie Tesoro Gaoing, Owner
Diplomat Tours and Travel

Hibiscus, state flower of Hawaii.

On strike I've lived together with local people. Ate three meals a day. I had to learn to use chopsticks. They have no inhibitions. Absolutely honest. No sham. If they liked you they made a point of letting you know they liked you. But the local people are changing. I think they're changing. I prefer the old days. . . . People are more greedy today than they were in the past. I don't think that it is because of the fight for higher wages. I think that the population has changed. A great influx of new immigrants from the Orient, Caucasians from the mainland, and people from the South Pacific, too. I don't know if Honolulu is losing its ability to assimilate people. After all, that's how Honolulu grew; but it appears to be more difficult living together now, than before. You're continually finding problems in the schools, which are in many instances based upon race. There was no "kill a haole day," 30 years ago.

Honolulu before the war was a place without any middle class — a bunch of haves and have-nots. You went out to Waikiki you didn't see a local boy, a local person in any of the hotels or the restaurants other than as menials — employees. As a matter of fact, it was the policy of most of the companies there not to hire Caucasians in certain jobs, because these jobs were considered to be jobs for non-Caucasians.

When Jack Hall and I organized the plantations the Oriental employees were frightened and intimidated. Remember when the plantation workers wore "bango" numbers? . . . There was no such thing as going into a large downtown store and having a charge account for a sugar worker. He bought at the company store and he was "bango" number so and so, and he was "hey you" by his supervisors. Now he's mister and she's missus. Probably the greatest thing the ILWU did for these people was to give them human dignity.

Robert McElrath, Regional Director, ILWU
Sugar and Pineapple Workers Union

We've had some strife in our labor relations, but not as much as the mainland. Some plantations did have some violence, but it was wrong-doing by management, there's no question about it. I recently looked at an old contract where they brought people out from Scotland. Now, you talk about discrimination against Filipinos and the Chinese, and how they were worked so hard; well, that contract with the Scots was pretty bad, too. It really tied them up. It was a tough contract. But I do think that the employers did have too much of a hold on plantation people. When you bought anything you bought from the company store. You know the old song, "You owe your life to the company store." Well, that was true. You owed your life to the plantation and the sugar factory, and there was something that had to be done about it and it was done.

John Bellinger, President
First Hawaiian Bank

Harvesting sugar cane on Oahu Sugar Company lands in Kunia.

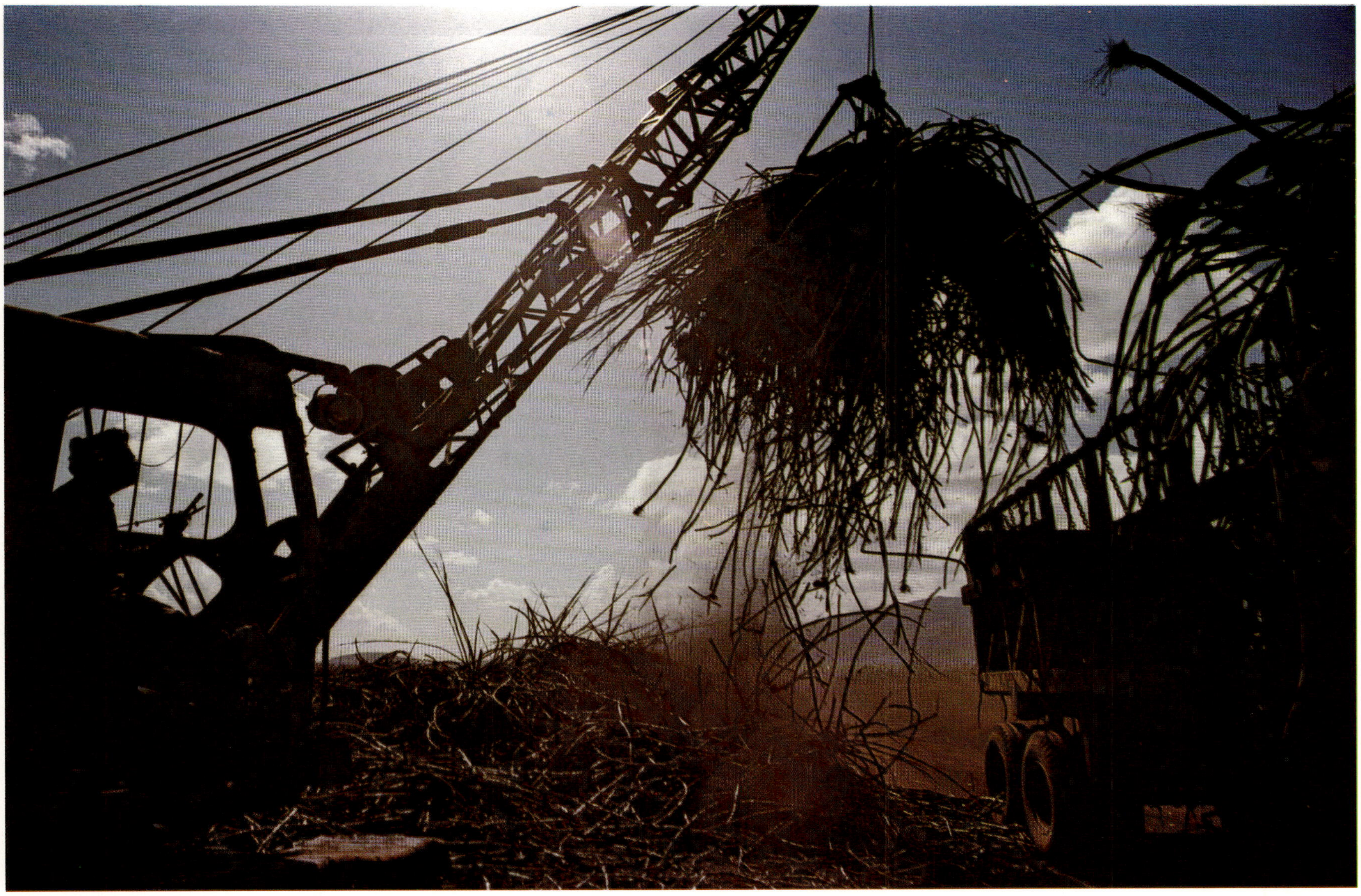

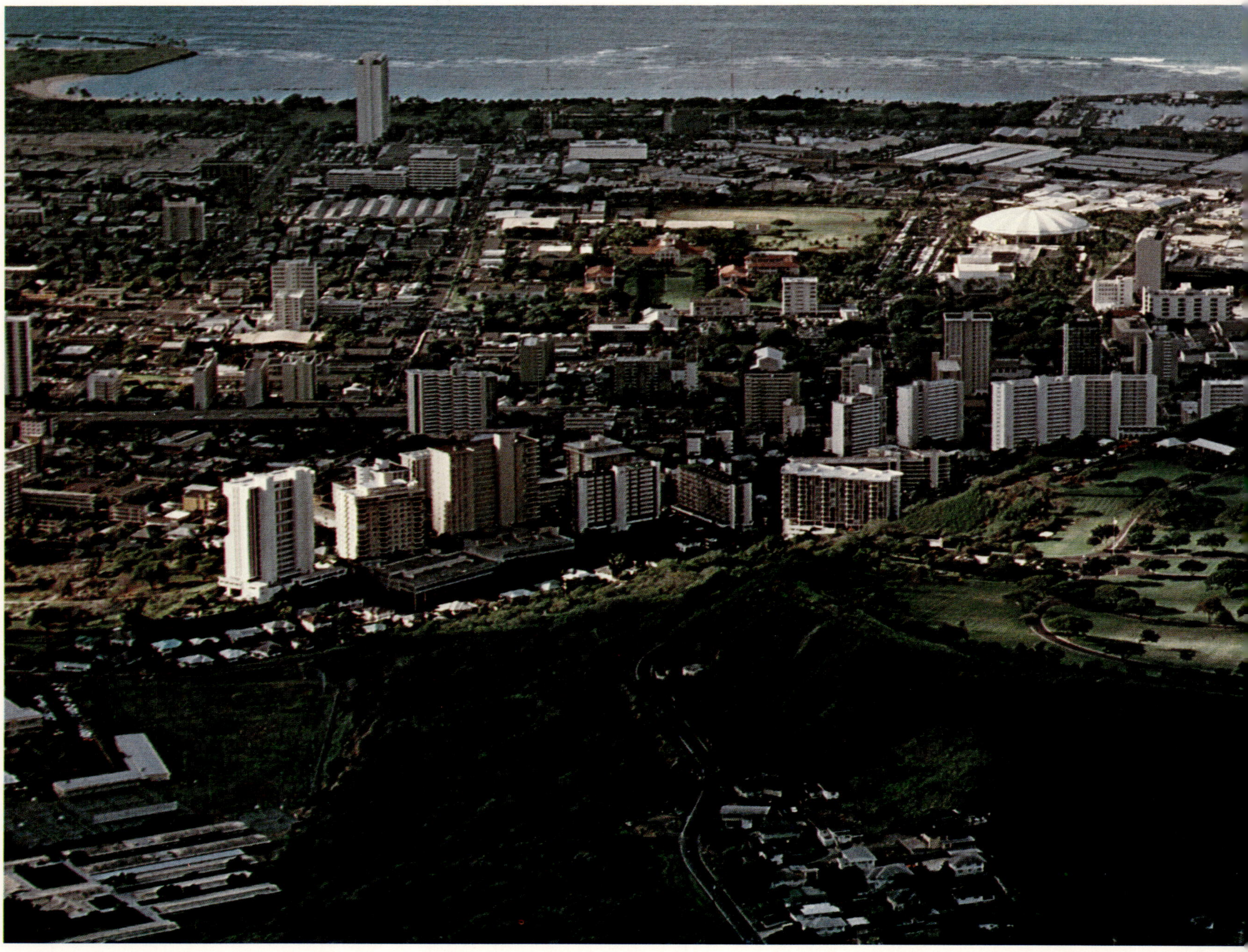

National Memorial Cemetery of the Pacific, in Punchbowl Crater. Called Puowaina in the old days, the name means a hill for placing human sacrifices, for which this crater was famous before the *kapu* system was abolished.

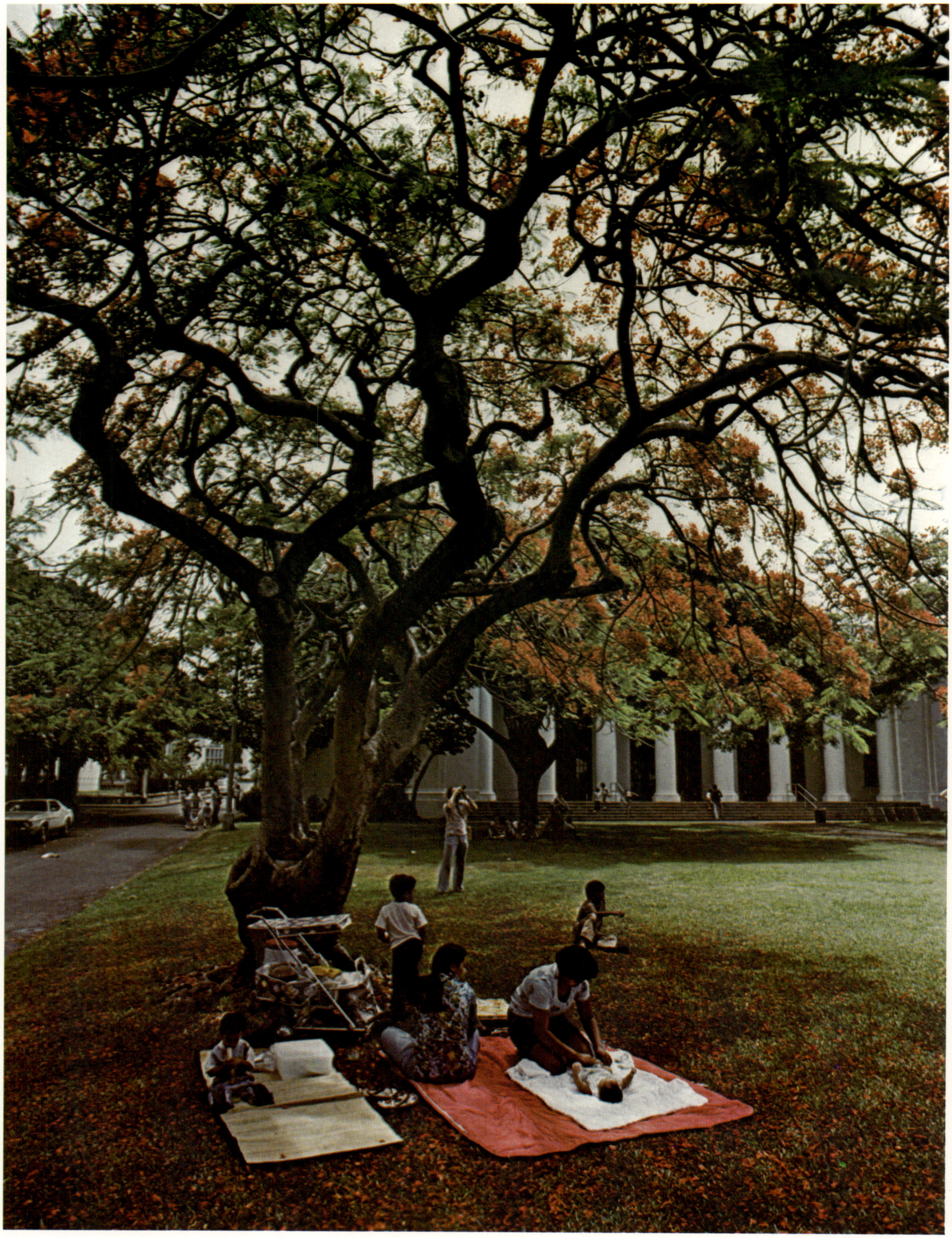

The Islands At War

I arrived in Honolulu on September 16, 1941, responding to a notice of civil engineering jobs available with the U. S. Army Corps of Engineers. I had sent them my educational résumé and within a week received a first-class ticket on Matson's *Lurline,* good one way to Hawaii. It was my first job.

I began work immediately, assigned to a drafting table in the converted top floor nightclub of the Alexander Young Hotel. The view from the top took in all of leeward Oahu from Diamond Head to the distant Wai'anae Mountains. Flat-topped Mt. Ka'ala dominated the far skyline and was the site of my first job assignment, to prepare construction drawings for a secret army radar installation atop the mountain. It would have clear electronic sightlines in all directions to detect far in advance any enemy aircraft that might approach Pearl Harbor.

There was considerable military activity during the following weeks, but not until November did anything unusual occur. On Sunday morning, the last day of November, 1941, I awoke to the noise of army tanks clattering along School Street, snaking in long lines across town behind truckloads of armed, helmeted troops. Hawaiian Electric's waterfront power plant was ringed by extra guards with fixed bayonets, gas masks ready. The entire Oahu military establishment had been placed on "sabotage" alert, a reduction in classification from the previous weeks "attack" status.

Governor John Burns, then a young police captain working closely with army G-2 and the FBI on espionage investigations, had learned of a probable attack on the U.S. by Japanese forces several days before December 7. The Honolulu FBI office head, Robert Shivers, had informed him in a private meeting, "We're going to be attacked before the week is out." Burns was curious why the military did not alert itself to attack if the FBI knew what was about to happen; but he prepared for the worst, placing his own espionage unit on alert for possible illegal information gathering and transmittal by Japanese residents — something that never occurred.

On the first day of December 1941, 72-year-old Governor Joseph Poindexter's M-Day Advisory Council, assuming a more relaxed attitude, said its "report is being built around the entire wartime preparedness picture in Hawaii," and was to be submitted to the governor for recommendations "this week."

On Saturday, December 6, the army on Oahu had been on "general alert" for over a week, the public mostly ignoring the military preparations. They assumed the activity to be routine military maneuvers that had been going on for some time. While the British recalled troops to their posts in Singapore, and the Philippine cabinet ordered all nonessential citizens out of Manila, Honolulu seemed more in tune with U.S. Senator Ralph Brewster of Maine, who said, "The U.S. Navy can defeat the Japanese Navy any place and at any time." We didn't even consider the possibility of a Japanese attack on "impregnable" Pearl Harbor. Saturday evening, American soldiers and sailors purchased tickets at the Waikiki Theater to enjoy the movie, *Yank in the RAF,* starring Tyrone Power and Betty Grable. To everyone at the time, the movie was the closest Hawaii would get to war. Some people made plans to hear the Twenty-seventh Infantry Division Band giving a concert at the Iolani Palace bandstand at 4:30 p.m. the next day, Sunday, December 7, 1941.

The only person in Honolulu who may have sensed something might be about to happen was local columnist James Chun, writing in the *Honolulu Star-Bulletin* for December 6. He wrote, "America and Japan are nearer the brink of war today than at any time since relations were established between the two countries by Commodore Matthew Perry."

I was up at 7:00 on Sunday morning to join the

I'm Scotch, English, Spanish, Portuguese and Hawaiian. My children are marrying and there's no concern about race. I don't have any concern about race either — never have had. I think that makes our golden people. I've been exposed to the opposite having traveled and lived on the mainland. I do know that prejudice does exist, that people are concerned about races and culture. When I was first introduced to this it startled me. I think for many of us brought up in Hawaii it's a blessing in disguise because our ignorance is bliss. A lot of times it probably has gotten me in trouble because I didn't even know what they were talking about, but I'm glad I didn't know. And, you know even my children don't know.

B. J. Feldman
Former Miss Hawaii

Family picnic on the lawn, downtown main branch, Library of Hawaii. Overleaf, the back side of Honolulu reveals a fluted *pali* for Kane'ohe and Kailua residents, a wilderness only minutes from downtown.

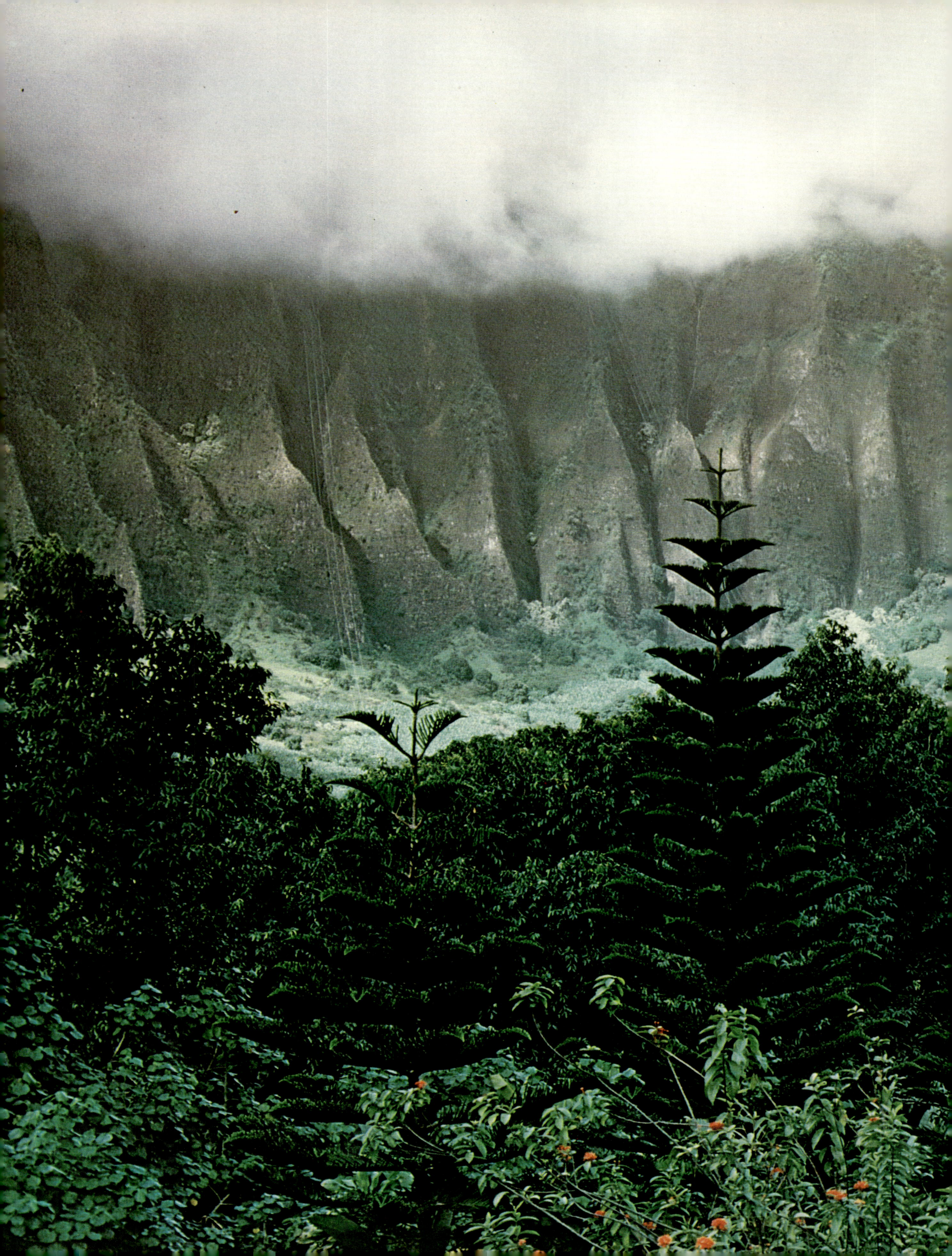

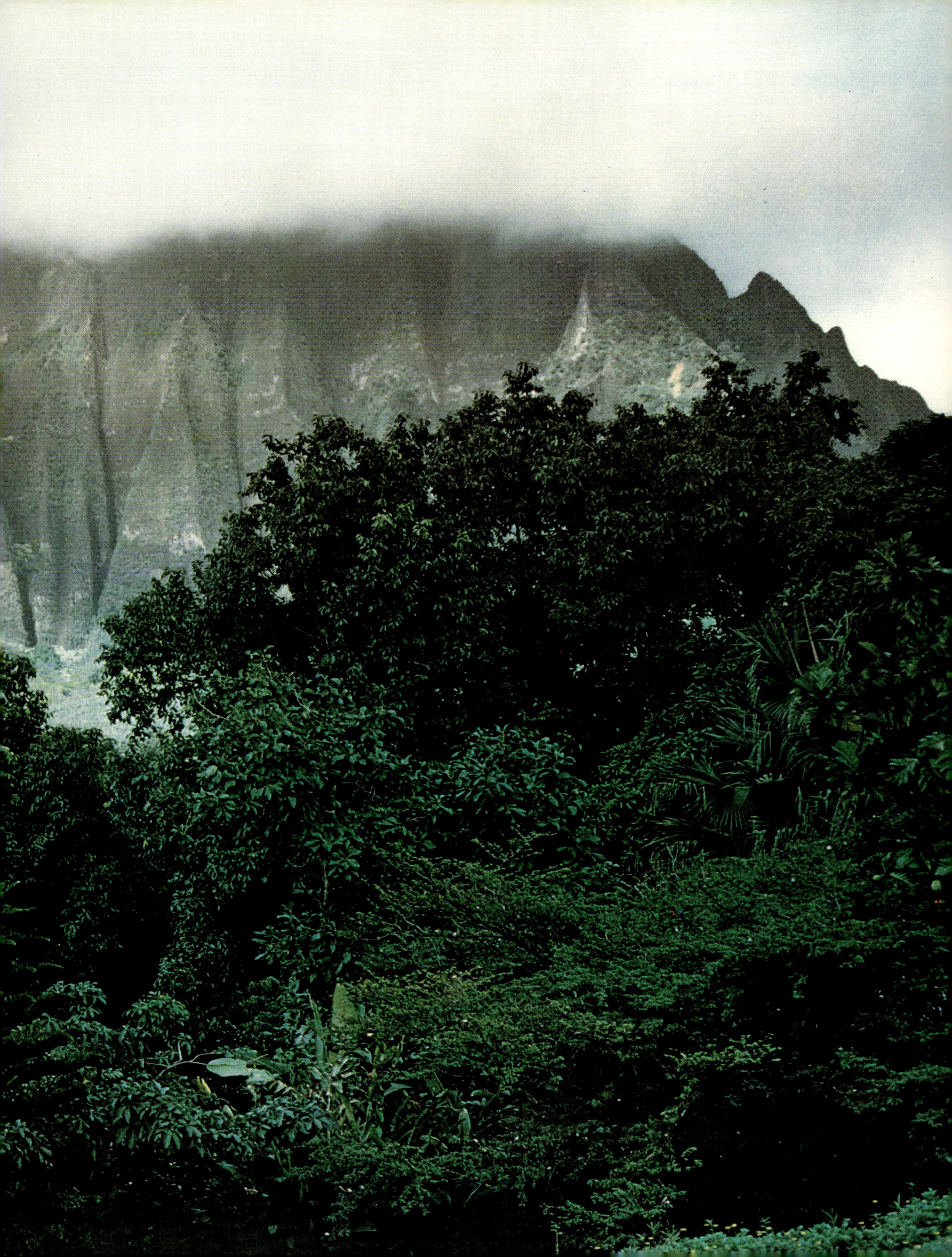

Hawaiian Trail & Mountain Club's scheduled hike down the long ridge above Mokuleiʻa, from Makua to Kaʻena Point. We gathered early at our regular meeting place, the downtown Army-Navy YMCA, because of the long drive across the island, and were on our way before 8:00, approaching Pearl Harbor, when we noticed several unusual aircraft overhead. I recognized the Japanese red "meatball" insignia at the same time I saw billowing clouds of black smoke over Pearl Harbor. This was obviously no elaborate naval rehearsal, so I changed my schedule for the day to walk the streets of Honolulu and see what happened. I had brought my small folding Kodak Retina with me for pictures on the trail. Perhaps I might photograph the beginning of the war if I could get close enough.

I left the car behind and walked up into residential Alewa Heights until I was sufficiently high for an unobstructed view over Pearl Harbor. It was like opening a page of *Life* magazine in full color, three dimensions, and sound. Seeing the rumble of distant explosions, black smoke mixed with splashes of bright orange, and small airplanes darting swiftly about was like watching an old war movie. Silver planes occasionally dived toward the earth and as quickly returned, into a sky peppered with small splotches that suddenly appeared, as if artist Jackson Pollock was creating a giant landscape by throwing buckets of black paint against the sky. It was frightening to watch.

As I stood with my mouth agape, asking myself what happens now, I heard the sound of a faint whistle, becoming louder and louder as it obviously moved closer. I took it to be the sound of falling bombs whistling in the air as they fell. Puffs of gray smoke rising above nearby homes, followed by muffled explosions, verified that the neighborhood was under attack and that I should find shelter. I looked around me, not knowing quite what to do, then I saw the flash of an explosion in the next block. Quickly I rolled into the nearest gutter, lying as flat as possible, as the whistling grew uncomfortably loud, heading directly toward me. The bomb exploded with a sharp bang in the middle of the street a few yards away, shrapnel pieces whistling outward in every direction. I heard them pass within inches of my ears and watched in amazement as the white paint of the wood cottage behind me instantly acquired dozens of black holes, the shrapnel spraying through the house like someone shaking black pepper on a baked potato. I didn't know the exposure, but I took some pictures, anyway.

I waited until I heard no more whistling and stood up, shaking dust and dirt off my hiking clothes. In the street, a new 1941 Packard sedan had stopped, its engine still running, a strange hum in an eerie silence. I walked over, curious, noting that the automobile, too, was punctured everywhere with the same black holes. I looked inside. The passengers had red holes and the man nearest me was trying to hold his arm together, the bone protruding from torn flesh. There was no way I could help them

I finished the roll of film in my camera and walked back down the hill. Several friends were waiting for me on the front *lanai* of my apartment on Judd Street and asked what I had seen. I started to tell them, but I could only open my mouth. I could not utter a sound. I was in shock and it was several hours before I was able to talk coherently about the beginning of the war.

On Monday I delivered my film to Wadsworth's Camera Shop for processing, and on Tuesday U.S. Navy Intelligence confiscated my film. When the next issue of *The Saturday Evening Post* magazine arrived in Honolulu, I saw my pictures spread across four pages, with captions telling of the death and destruction by the Japanese bombing of Honolulu. They were not my captions, but they were my first published photographs.

Most of the other hikers tried to continue, but police turned them back before they reached Pearl Harbor. One group, which left early to meet friends in Wahiawa, was surprised when no one else arrived at the trailhead, then did the hike anyway, enjoying the trail by themselves, unaware that anything unusual had happened until they returned home to a curfew and blackout.

Newspapers and radio were a mixture of rumors and unverified reports of enemy landings and sabotage. Japanese parachutists were said to have made night

Hawaiian music will be around a long, long time. In many respects, it's all we have left. I live in Waikiki, and every time I look out my window and see all the high rises and buildings, it makes me sick. But when I sit down and start playing a song that's survived for 100 years or so, it makes me feel better.

Eddie Kamae, musician
Sons of Hawaii

Two opposing cultures meet in Waikiki at the corner of Kalakaua and Ohua.

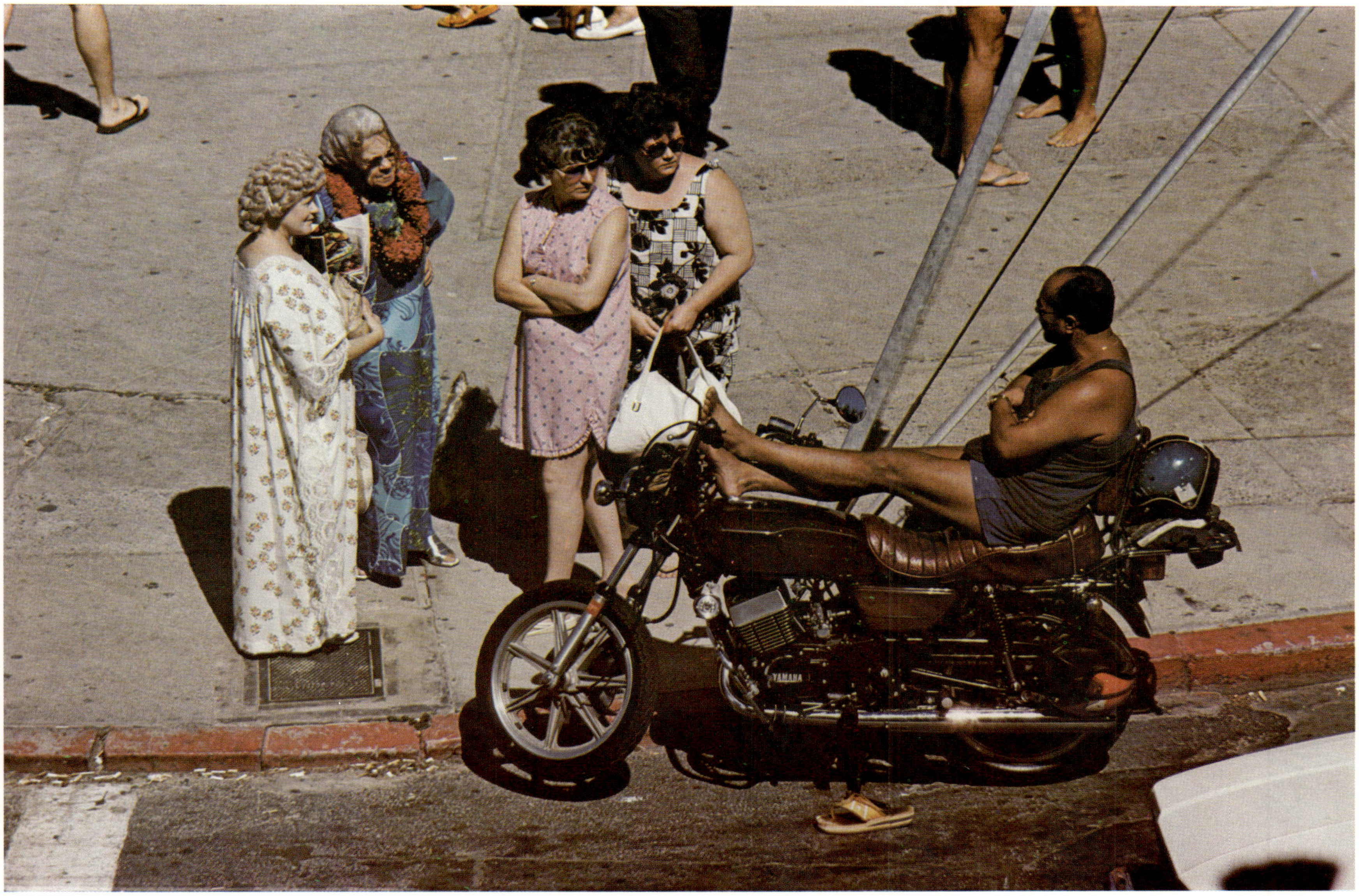
YAMAHA

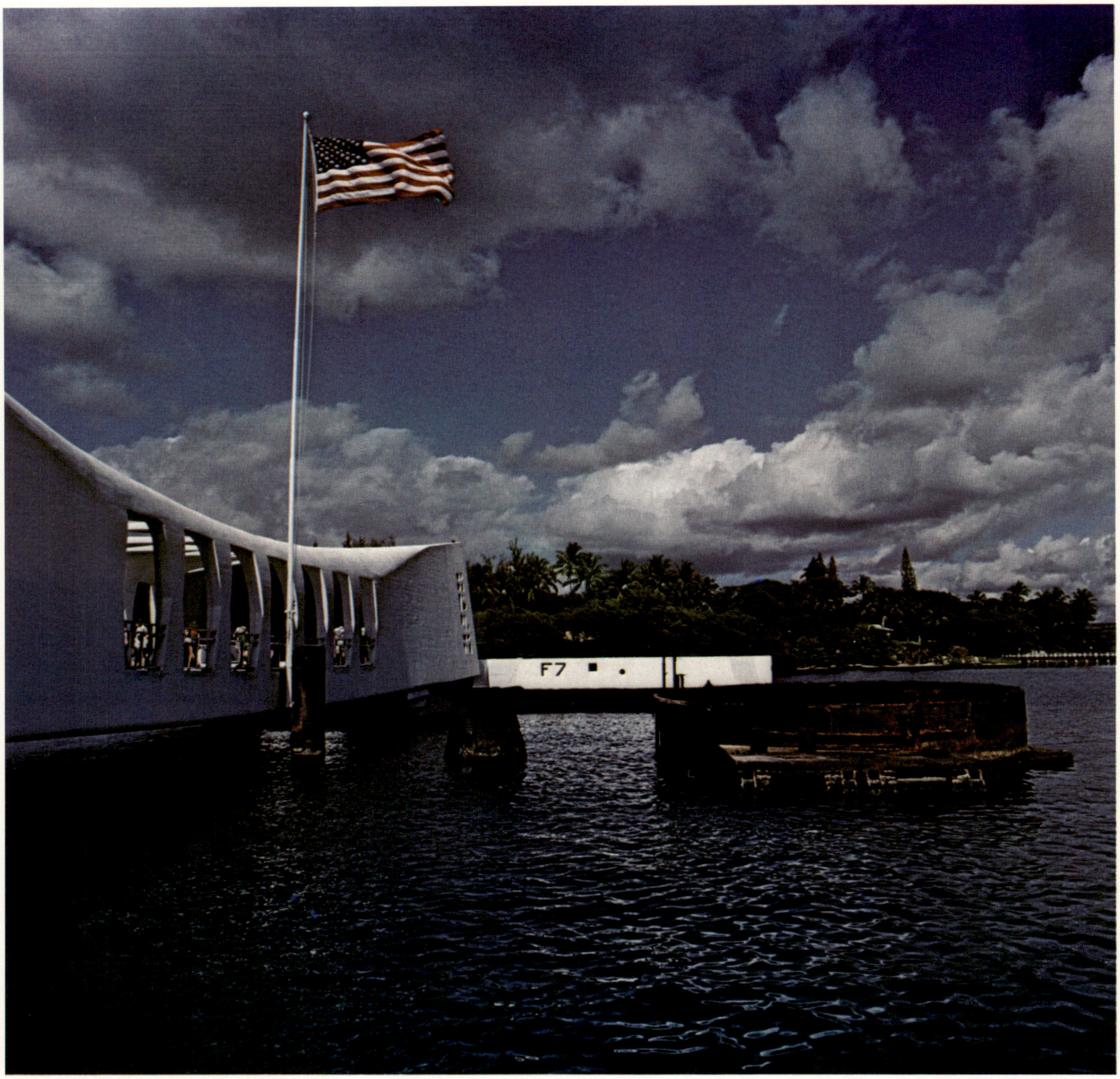
F7

landings and were waiting in hiding for a follow-up invasion expected at any time. The next morning, when planes from U.S. aircraft carriers flew in to land at Ford Island, jittery Pearl Harbor gunners opened fire again until calmer heads got things quieted down.

Monday morning I was notified to report with others to Kewalo Basin and help scuttle fishing sampans used by local Japanese fishermen — before their vessels could be used to refuel submarines reportedly cruising offshore. I thought the request was silly and refused to go. The request was typical of the strange behavior of otherwise reasonable adults that occurred often while the military slowly pulled itself together again.

Next day, in the early morning hours of Tuesday, one of my army engineer bosses, Colonel Theodore Wyman, started out with a truck convoy, headed for the University of Hawaii in lower Monoa Valley. His orders were to take over the university buildings to accommodate a rapidly expanding engineering staff (soon to triple in size). He drove out Wilder Street in the blackout, headed toward the Manoa campus, not quite sure where he was, looking for the identifying concrete gateposts at the university entrance. Nearing Manoa Valley, his car headlights reflected off the bronze plaques reading Oahu College.

Assured that he had arrived at the university, Wyman, who should have known better, pushed through the entrance gates, disregarding protestations of the night watchman, and took over the campus in the name of the Corps of Engineers. Not having keys, he broke open doors to buildings and moved out furniture and personal belongings, replacing school books with engineering manuals. The centrally located auditorium was divided by scaffolding into two floors, and my drafting table was removed from downtown to a high-level perch on the newly built second floor of Dillingham Hall.

When the faculty and students of Punahou School arrived in the morning, unaware their school had been occupied, they protested since it was clearly evident to them that the army had made a mistake in the dark and had occupied the wrong campus. The army steadfastly denied any error, but it was not until two days later that official notice was received by the Punahou president. Punahou students moved to the university and we stayed at Punahou for the duration of the war, until the Corps of Engineers constructed its own headquarters building at Fort Armstrong. The name of Oahu College had been changed to Punahou School seven years before, but unfortunately no one had gotten around to changing the entrance nameplates.

On the first day of March 1942, two Japanese Nakajima four-engined long-range flying boats took off from Wotje Island in Micronesia, flying to French Frigate Shoals in the Hawaiian Leeward chain. Landing on the quiet lagoon, the aircraft taxied slowly to waiting Japanese submarines, where they were quietly refueled

Kane'ohe Marine Corps Air Station.

I always think of the definition of Honolulu — fairhaven. In the days when we were growing up with the steamers, and now, of course, the planes taking the place of the steamers, it's still fairhaven. In spite of all the growth and the modern buildings and all, I think that Honolulu still has a welcoming feeling to it, a warmth; that, perhaps, is taken care of by the sea, the sky and the mountains, regardless of what man has done to pollute the landscape.

R. Alex Anderson, Composer
Lovely Hula Hands, Mele Kalikimaka

Arizona Memorial, Pearl Harbor.

and loaded with 500-pound fragmentation bombs. The next evening they were again in the air, this time on a direct course to Honolulu.

On the same evening, March 4, four employees of the Corps of Engineers, including myself, who had together rented a single large house on Pacific Heights, were hosting a typical "curfew" party of the time. Since our war restrictions prohibited late night travel, it was common to hold all-night parties, because no one could go home anyway and it was unnecessary to limit liquor consumption. Liquor and gasoline were the only items rationed in Hawaii, but there was always plenty of wine and whiskey. The parties were often rambunctious affairs, and our house, with three floors of rooms, provided many opportunities for varied activities. Windows on the first two floors were blacked out with opaque paper because martial law's General Orders prohibited lights that could be seen from the street. Even lighted cigarettes and pipes were prohibited unless an actual attack was underway.

We kept our top floor, with its broad *lanais* and large sliding glass doors, clear and open, so we could always see the great panoramic view we enjoyed from Diamond Head to Pearl Harbor. The night of our party was no exception, and groups of laughing couples would, on occasion, venture up the stairs to dance a little or simply sit quietly holding hands, looking over the dark city spread below. The blacked-out city always held a fascination for me, as it lay stretched out in front of the house, sound asleep, with seldom a sign of activity or movement. The city was always very still, without night auto traffic, and it was fun to imagine what went on in the darkness. Only sporadic shafts of light from army searchlights trying to find something in the sky would interrupt the silent nights.

Every 15 minutes or so I would climb upstairs with my flash camera to photograph friends in our "open" room, not worrying too much about any possible blackout violation because, after all, the light wasn't on very long! As was the usual procedure, around midnight everyone gradually went to sleep, scattered here and there on every floor in the house. I flashed a few more photographs of sleeping couples before finding my own bedroom.

At what seemed like only minutes later, we were awakened by loud pounding on every door in the house. Before we could reply, doors were broken open and army soldiers, holding rifles with bayonets, crowded into the house. Moving from top to bottom they quickly herded us together in the kitchen and an officer stepped forward. We were all half-asleep and irritated at being suddenly awakened. But our aggravation was partially relieved by the knowledge they were *our* soldiers.

The officer asked who was responsible for the "coded light signals being sent from this house." We pointed out that all of us were civilian employees of the Corps of Engineers and were not spies. None of us were sending signals. He said the command post atop Diamond Head had been recording light signals from our house for several hours. There was no mistake. I then remembered my flash photography. That was it! The intermittent use of flash could easily be interpreted as signals from a distance. I brought out my camera and explained what had happened. We were sorry, but none of us had any idea my flashes would be seen by someone who might try to decode them. (I've always wondered what the message was.) The army squad was convinced they had uncovered a nest of spies, and were disappointed on learning we were merely a bunch of drunk engineers. They took my camera to process the film for proof that I was indeed taking flash pictures, and departed, offering apologies for breaking the door. We all went back to bed again.

An hour later a trembling boom practically knocked me out of bed. I ran to open the door before anyone else broke it down, and saw a bright orange flash in Pauoa Valley below followed quickly by another boom that shook the house, then a third behind Punchbowl Ridge near Roosevelt High School. I knew what was down there in the dark — I had designed the sewer and water systems for two army camps in the area. Behind Punchbowl was a

---

I'm sorry we had to go to the high rise condominiums. So many of our people who always lived in houses with yards now have to live in apartments, especially the young people, but I understand that we just don't have that much land. For myself I just don't dig those 20 and 30 story things. I just can't imagine not being able to hang clothes on a clothesline and walk barefoot in the grass.

B. J. Feldman
Former Miss Hawaii

Kolekole Pass Road in the Wai'anaes, carries military traffic across the island between the Navy's Lualualei Ammunition Depot and the Army's Schofield Barracks.

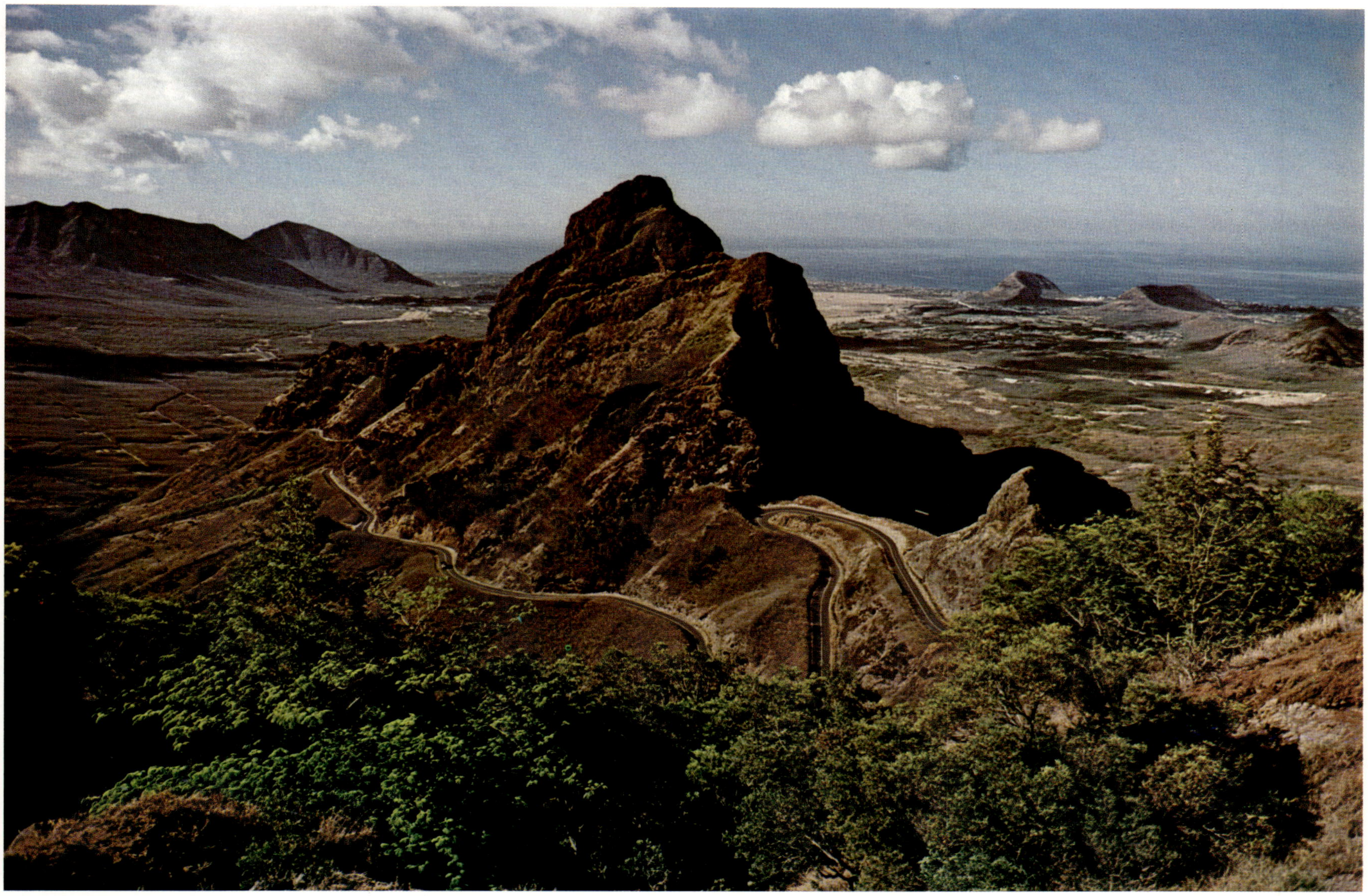

light tank battalion, and in upper Pauoa Valley was a battery of 16-inch mortars. I'm sure the commanding officers of those units felt the Japanese bomber was right on target.

I heard a siren somewhere after searchlights came on, stabbing the dark sky, trying to locate the distant sound of a high-flying multi-engine aircraft overhead in the night. The entire house was now awake, rushing to the "open" top to see what was happening. Most of us were probably wondering how we would *now* explain our "flash signals" to army intelligence. The bombs were real and the bomber flew right over our house.

On the way to work in the morning I visited the Pauoa mortar battery. The bombs hadn't hit anything important, except the latrine I had designed. The commanding officer, unshaven and a little disheveled, had apparently been informed of the raid on our house just before the bombs fell and showed me fragments of the bomb with Japanese inscriptions. He implied quite strongly that it was probably all my fault. I hardly knew how to reply, but did mumble a sort of "I'm sorry." It's the only time I ever apologized for a bombing.

Our work intensified in the weeks ahead, with many overtime hours on top secret underground installations. Oahu was preparing to outlast an expected Japanese siege of many months, and all the necessary military hardware was being removed to vast underground tunnels. A complete three-story aircraft assembly plant, power units, long-range radio facilities, and millions of gallons of ship bunker oil and aircraft gasoline were placed underground in excavated caverns.

When we learned a Japanese battle fleet with troop transports was approaching Midway, it was evident the success of our work would be soon tested. The entire population was aware of the forthcoming battle, understood its significance, and watched with concern as soldiers and sailors disappeared from Waikiki and downtown brothels on River Street. It seemed that most of our aircraft flew north, and the public "grapevine" of battle information seemed to verify the fact that many did not return. Defense workers had finished repairing the carrier *Enterprise* in record time, and she left Pearl Harbor without fanfare, also headed north. No fighting ships of any consequence remained. Island activity stopped after the intensive effort of past weeks. We were almost all government employees, so even with censorship, the word passed quickly about battle progress. It was quite evident we had broken the Japanese code, because most of our Pacific Fleet fighting forces were waiting near Midway. For most of us there was little to do except wait. We had given the soldiers, sailors, and marines all we had. Now, it was up to them. The battle was joined.

It was Sunday in early June, during the last days of the Battle of Midway, when I joined the scheduled Hawaiian Trail & Mountain Club hike to Sacred Falls in the Koʻolaus back of Hauʻula. The trail begins at a narrow cleft in the hills, where a clear water stream exits from its underground mountain source. We hopped back and forth between boulders in the stream to keep our feet dry, gradually moving farther and farther into the mountain, where the black lava walls are close together, until the stream suddenly ended against a vertical cliff. The gulch there is only about a hundred feet wide, and a steady flow of water dropped from the *pali* above into a small, rocky pool. We lounged quietly for several hours, eating our lunches, occasionally looking straight overhead, where jagged upper edges of the gulch opened to the sky in a narrow crack that almost sealed us off from the rest of the world. Perhaps in a way we had escaped into the earth for a short respite; into ourselves where contemplation of the fierce battle raging outside was made easier to understand.

Walking into Sacred Falls we passed large boulders with piles of three smaller rocks atop each other. Beneath the smaller rocks were remains of old leaves, sometimes with only the dry-vein skeleton remaining. They were offerings to the pig god, *puaʻa*. We prepared our own offerings, placing three small pebbles atop an avocado leaf so the gods would not permit any rocks to fall on us from the *pali* overhead. None did.

It was a pleasant day inside the mountain, away from the world. But upon returning outside, with the windward hills already in late afternoon shade, we found an even better world waiting for us. The Battle of Midway was over and we had won. ∎

Honolulu is a great place to live, everything's convenient. There's a lot of things going on too, but too much violence. The high buildings, okeh as it is now. They might just as well leave it like it is, but just stop building more and leave it like how it is now.

Matthew Tavares
Parking lot attendant

Tasseled sugarcane, Waipahu.

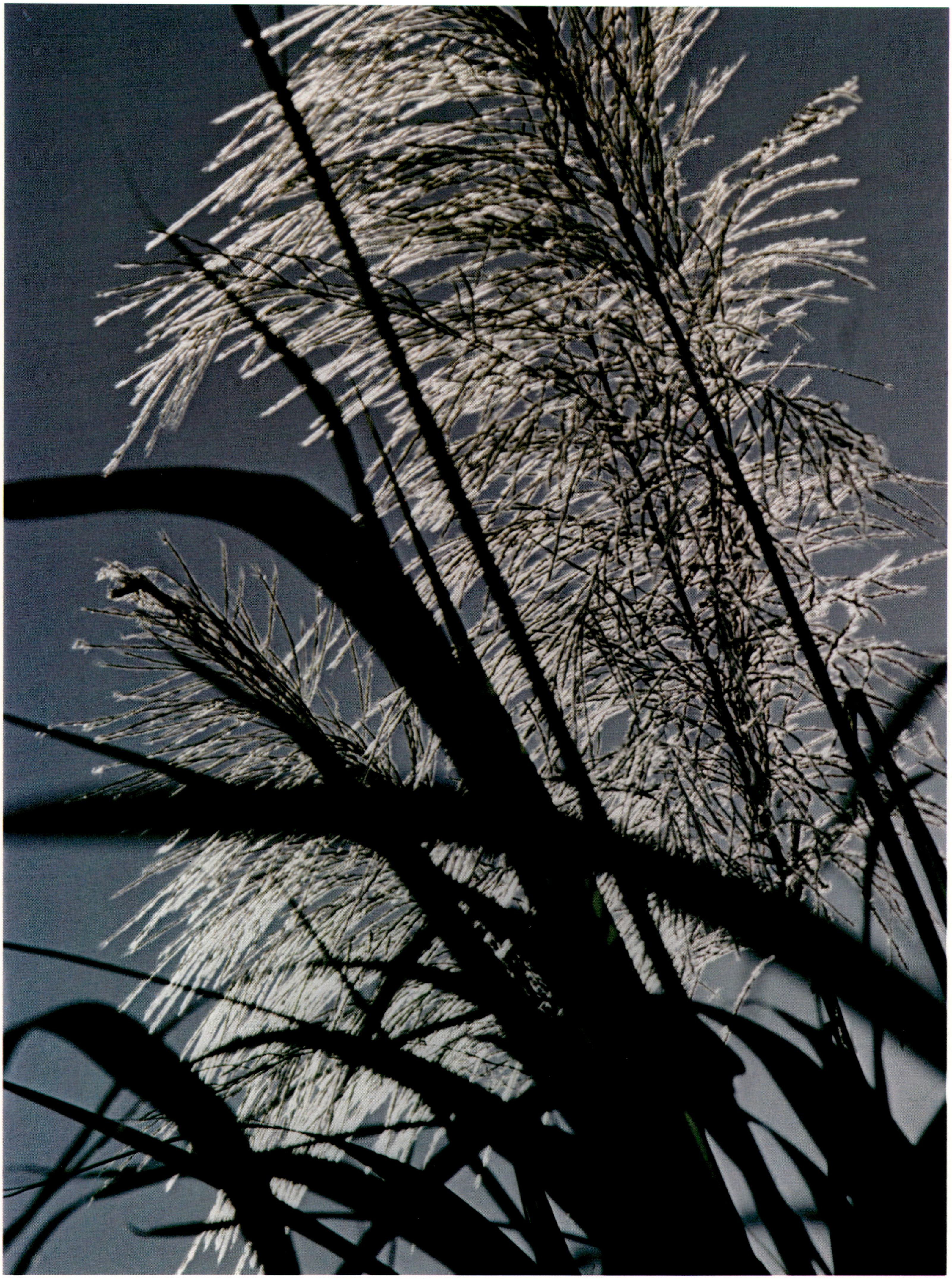

Hawaii Kai, 1978.

When Henry Kaiser first saw the old Hawaiian Kuapa fishponds, still being used for raising mullet in 1960, he could think of little else than progress: how to dredge, fill, and subdivide them into the Hawaii Kai of today. It was believed by some that *menehunes* built the pond, working only at night and connecting the pond by a tunnel to Ka'elepulu Pond near Kailua.

Hawaii Kai, 1960.

I was born in New York, but I traveled all around the country. Went through school in San Francisco. A guy on board a ship saw me on the street one day and asked me if I wanted to take a trip to Hawaii, and I said when? He said this afternoon. I said OK. So, I came over here. . . . I had been here several times on ships as a musician, and I enjoyed Honolulu. I wasn't doing anything and I thought it would be a great change for me to be warm. I figured if I was going to starve to death I might as well be warm, y'know. So, I came and I stayed. . . .

I always refer to the mainland on the air as "America." Honolulu isn't really like "America," even today, just because of the people who live here. A third are haoles, a third are Japanese and a third are all mixed up – in different colors. And the real thrill, even though maybe it's sublimal with the tourists, is to see all these different kinds of complexions working together, living together, studying together. And nobody has any real problems. Not like in "America."

When I first got here after the war, I think there were two restaurants in Waikiki. One was the old Moana Hotel restaurant that was out on the pier out over the ocean. It was run by Matson. It was a good place to eat. The food was good. And the other place was called the Waikiki Tavern. God help us. They had a cafeteria and they had two dishes — greasy mahimahi *and greasy liver and bacon. And that's all they ever served, except for beans, I guess. There were no street restaurants in Waikiki at the time. Now, of course, I think I could name off 50 magnificent restaurants. Any cuisine you like. You can spend as much or as little as you want. I go everywhere, from places like Bagwells, The Third Floor, Canlis, Michel's. I can't remember all the high-class joints. To places like Seikya's, where you get, y'know, the Japanese hamburgers, the* sushi, *and all that stuff across from Kaimuki High School. Or King's Bakery. Or Coco's — used to be Kau Kau Korner. Or the old days of the Smile Cafe or The New Eagle, which is still around. And today I still eat all the way from those high-class joints down to these kind of, well, hash houses, y'know, one-arm joints like Ono Hawaiian Food with six tables, but very good.*

J. Akuhead Pupule, disc jockey, KGMB
Self-proclaimed legend in his own time

Well, Honolulu it gotta change, yeah? Everyplace gotta change, yeah? So, everybody move with the tide — with the change, too.

Sam Kanehailua
Carpenter, Nanakuli

Waikiki Beach, summer 1978, the tourist years.

Waikiki Beach, spring 1942, the war years.

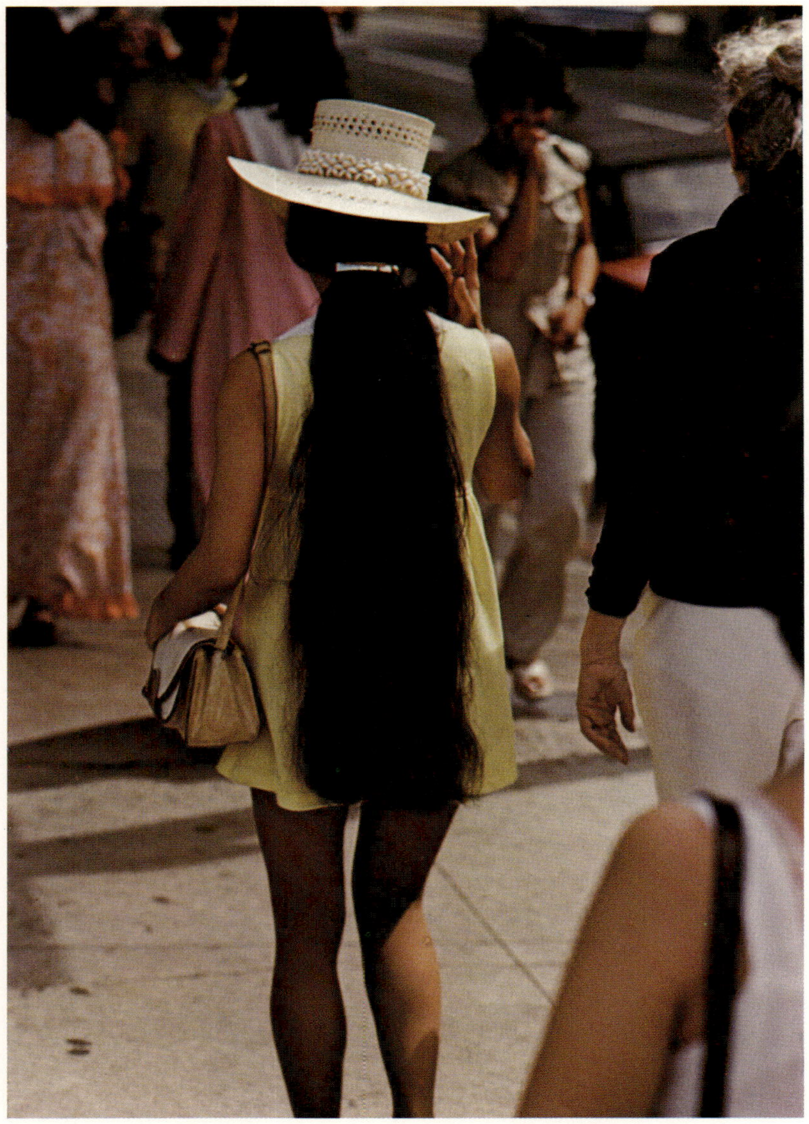

We Made It A Good Town

Growing up with Honolulu is an adventure story, replete with suspense, romance and excitement. The island changed considerably in the process, emerging from its tropical cocoon into the modern world, to grow rapidly into a mature city and state, yet somehow still retaining much of the gentle small town feeling first encountered upon my arrival, three months before the bombing of Pearl Harbor.

I had no premonition of the violent event soon to occur, nor was I aware at the time of the revolutionary social changes already begun by different individuals I was yet to meet, some of whom I would strongly oppose in days to come, and others — both *kama'ainas* and new immigrants like myself — whom I would join to help create a new social and physical environment on a group of islands that would eventually become the fiftieth state. The experience has been immensely satisfying, for I was able to actively be involved in the changes that directly affected the eventual character and physical appearance of Honolulu. I had always urged citizen participation, and while my part in most instances was probably a minor role — I was just pushing a little, with many others — it is clear in retrospect, and an exciting contemplation, that I may have made a difference in some cases.

It is always difficult to determine who has cast the deciding vote. Given the normal inertia of events, much might have happened anyway, but I see little that may have occurred without the urging by personalities who wanted it to happen. As a political advocate and an active environmentalist, it has been possible for me to experience the failures, where growing up resulted in painful dislocations, and, in my opinion, some unfortunate mistakes. I see them everywhere — a missing banyan tree, high-rise hotels where none should be, subdivisions in cane fields, and a lost lake. But I find few mistakes in the economic and social community that we created. I'm pleased with the results. Honolulu grew quickly from territorial status into statehood with few serious traumatic incidents along the way, generally escaping the worst with only a few scratches. We made it a good town to live in.

Postwar Honolulu could be accurately described as a "plantation town." It bore none of the visual appearances ordinarily associated with traditional company towns; but its dependence on a single economic oligarchy was quite typical of the time.. It was called the "Big Five," and its corporate family control over sugar, pineapple, shipping, and politics was complete.

Many attempts had been made to organize the plantations in past years, but all failed, with the strikes generally being organized and broken along racial lines. It wasn't until union organizers from Harry Bridges, San Francisco-based longshoremen's union (ILWU) arrived in Hawaii, that organization of the sugar and pineapple plantations on an industry-wide base was accomplished after World War II. The first sugar strike called by the ILWU was, more than anything else, to achieve union recognition.

On the first morning of the strike, I drove the union's regional director, Jack Hall, across the island to Waialua, where he delivered an almost revolutionary speech to Waialua sugar workers. Hall was quite nearsighted and had difficulty driving, so I took "annual leave" from my government engineering job and volunteered to chauffeur him to three different plantation strike rallies. It was my first actual meeting of island plantation workers, and I was amazed with the offhanded way they had occupied sugar company property; the company gymnasium at Waipahu had been taken over as strike headquarters, without any apparent attempt by the company to evict them. Neither was there ever any serious move to reopen the sugar mills with strikebreakers. I was deeply impressed by this unusual relationship between employer and union, and could not help but compare the relative peacefulness of this Hawaiian strike with the

---

Anyone moving to Honolulu is moving into one of the best cities in the United States — maybe the world. His children will have an equal educational opportunity in this state which he may not have on the mainland. Our school money is appropriated by the legislature and is not collected from property in a ghetto area which might be very low or in a wealthy Beverly Hills. Here we allocate our money equally irrespective of the income in a school district . . . Honolulu is the example I hope someday all America will follow . . . It's the Aloha spirit we have — no other place has it.

Charles Clark, Superintendent
State Department of Education

Legal secretary on her lunch hour, Fort Street, downtown Honolulu. Overleaf, Halona Cove on a quiet Sunday afternoon. One of the last volcanic eruptions on Oahu poured lava into the ocean from Koko Crater at Halona.

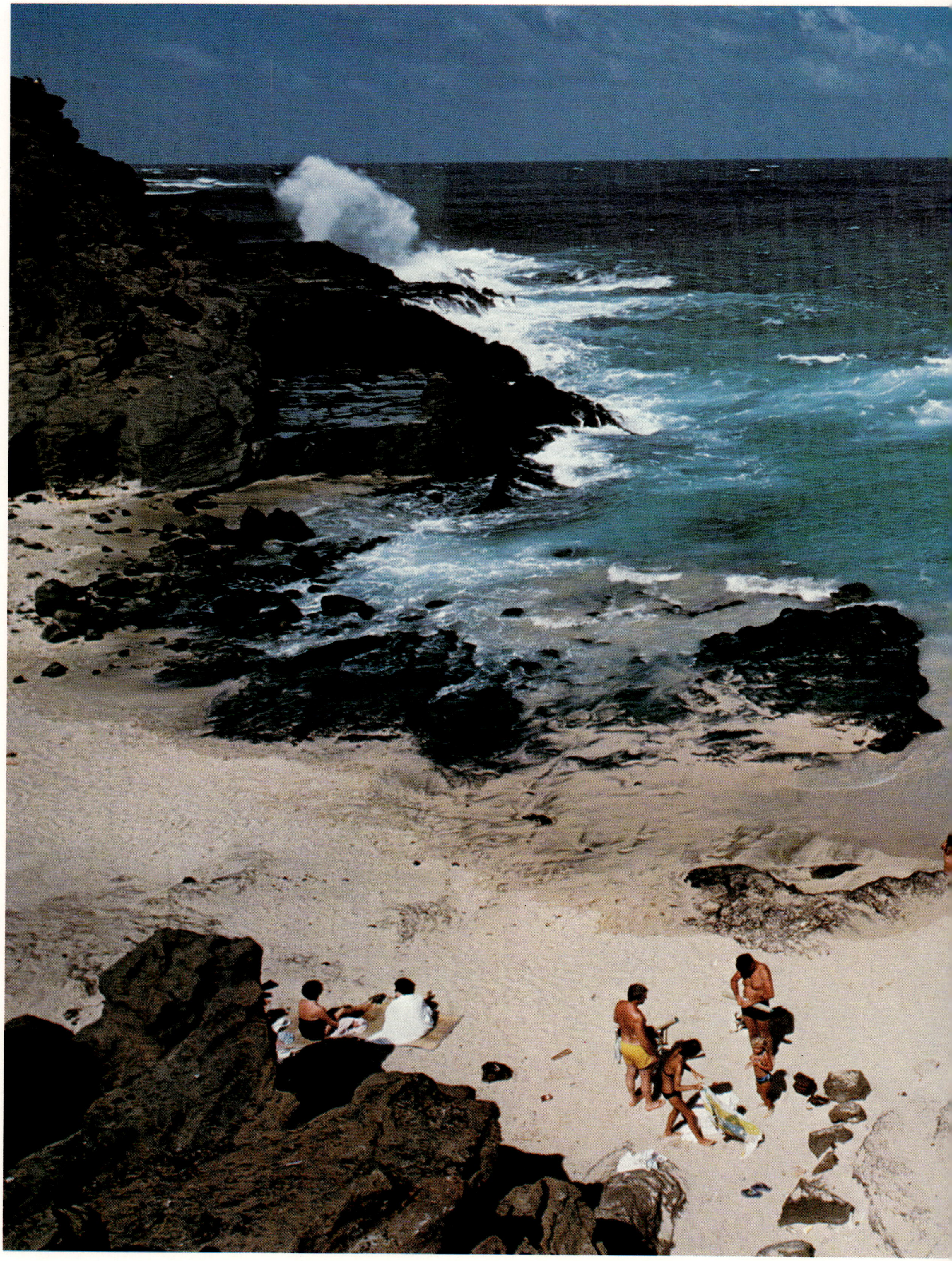

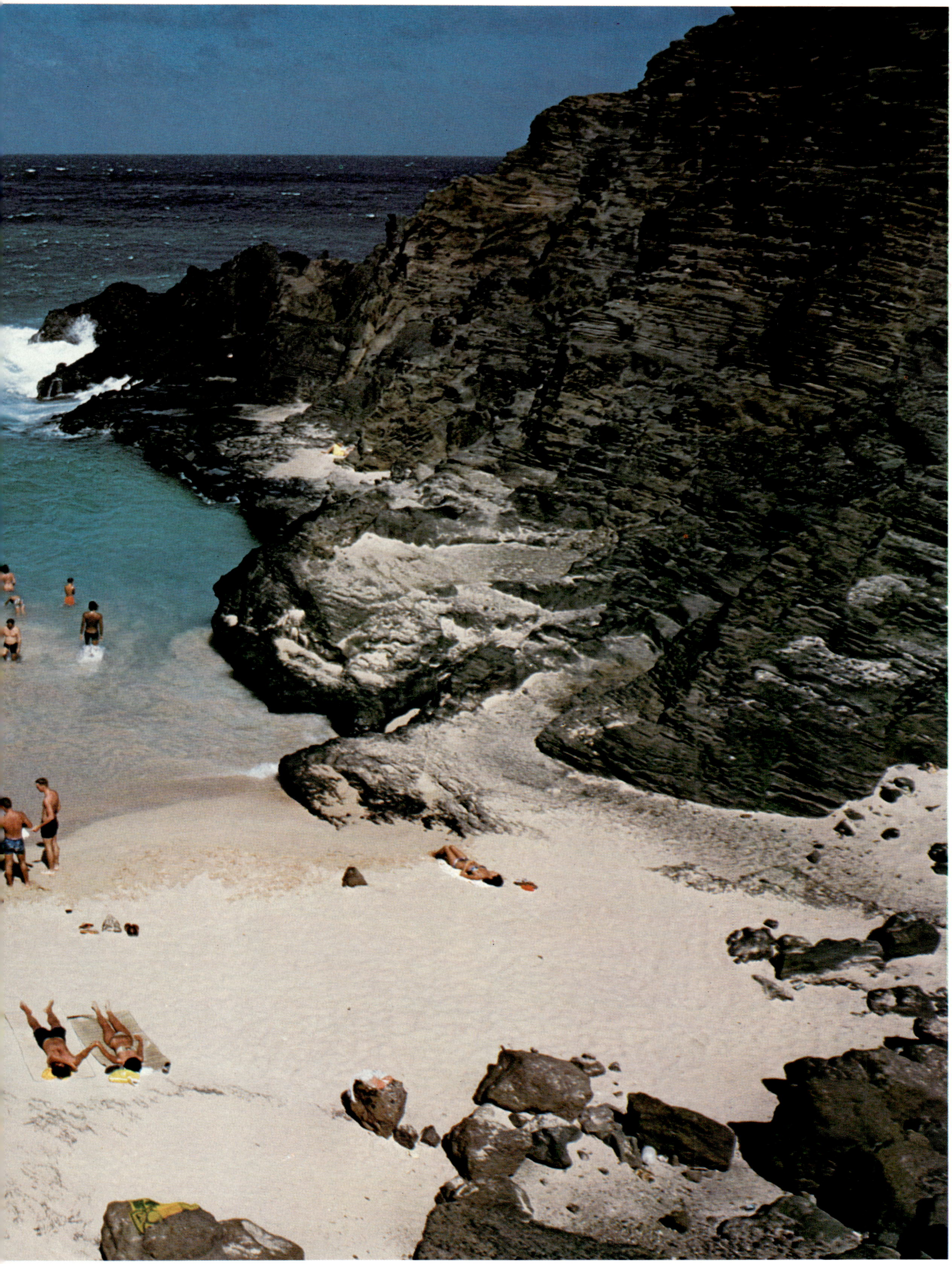

My parents born Japan. I'm second generation. We lived in Kipu, Kauai and in the morning they bakes, takes care of the bakery and work on the sugar plantation for Charlie Rice. In the morning they do the baking, early in the morning. Then go out and work on the plantation — take all the kids, and then come back and start selling the pastries that he baked. That's how he get enough money, y'know, to start his own business, a chop suey house on Fort Street. They hire one Chinese cook and they learned as they paying him, y'see. My wife and I, we started with four tables. I'm the cook and my wife is the waitress. My parents purchased this property. From there, just keep going, eh? I could see that catering was going to be a big type of business, so we started with one station wagon doing this international type of food. Today we sell all kinda food, like Filipino, Japanese, Chinese food, Hawaiian food, Portuguese food, and so forth. But you have to learn all those things from your friends. Like my father knew that if you know people they would teach you. So, Johnny Wilson, he used to be Mayor, the wife, from them we learn how to cook Hawaiian food. So, to learn things it takes friends.

But in all kinda food or culture or so forth, like the oriental, you are born with certain talent, so you learn the basic thing when you use your common sense. So, for example when you kalua a pig, 'cause I'm a Japanese they say I don't know how to kalua a pig. I say, look, brudda, the main thing is you make the stone hot and put 'em inside the pig stomach in the right place. Then you cook the pig. That's the main thing. That's the kind challenge I gotta go through.

Before when you make a luau you go to the mountain and get a pig. Go down the ocean and get the fish and the limu. You can get the flowers in the mountains, too. You can get this and you can get that. As time keep going they all keep coming in Honolulu, so in Honolulu they say, chee, we don't have this an we don't have that, because not too much island here and everyday people is going into the ocean. So, what we do, call Kauai, Maui, Molokai. You can't get the stuff in Honolulu so easy. So, now you gotta have friends on the different islands. Now people gotta get their own things, like opihi. They very expensive — one gallon about $100 it costs. But there's different type of opihi. You want the good one. That's the one that stay in the limu. The thing is orange. When you chew 'em the milk comes out. Same thing with squid. That's a seasonal thing. The legislature is trying to control those things like opihi because some people just goes and pick opihi and just throws the meat away and just sell the shell for jewelry business, and that's how we running out of opihi.

And like the pig. The Hawaiians, they kill the pig, they take the blood and they take a certain part and they feed that to the workers — the pipe, the intestines, na'au and loko. But the Federals say you cannot use that part. But they don't understand the culture and the food and so forth. Local people, wearing nice clothes, they get good job. They go down Ala Moana, eat plate lunch. They don't go fancy restaurant and sit down, all the linen and so forth, because they were born eating that certain kind food like stew and rice with a hot dog or maybe spare rib, 'eh? So, like when you go into real deep Hawaiian food, like crab, loko (that's that liver), other people say, we don't eat that stuff. They don't eat 'em. But then when you take all that raw stuff out — they eat 'em.

Tourists we cater to fit their mouths and their taste, because if you don't the crowds get less and less. Poi gotta be there, little bit. Now let's say a person go back home, it's say in Chicago, New York, Tokyo. Their friends ask did you eat that thing just like paste? Little story you see. But you have to feed them not too authentic. You have to make 50-50, half authentic and so much other kind. Let me see, before it used to be poi in the lau. Now in there we have ophi, haupia, luau chicken, laulau, baked banana, green onion, Hawaiian salt and limu. And we had sweet potato, lomi salmon, cake. But today we give 'em steak, one small piece mahimahi (gotta put fish inside there), fried rice, the poi, the salmon still there yet, the pineapple gotta be there, and the cake plus fried chicken — southern fried chicken. They love it. We make any kind food you want.

Ted Kaneda
Kaneda Catering

The "Hawaiian" garden by tradition is not too well organized, but a place where you stick something in the ground and stand back. Wai'anae.

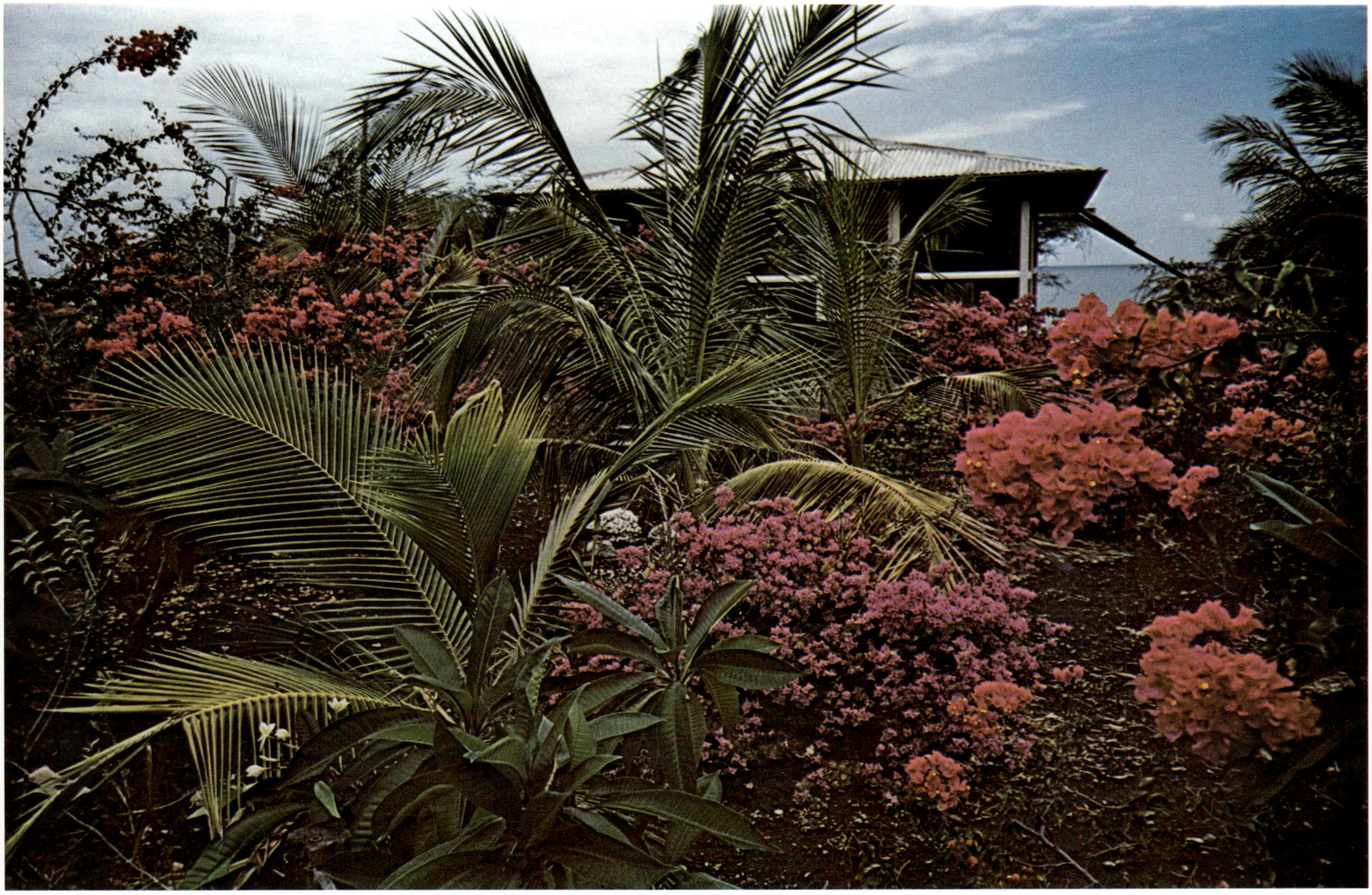

End of the island, the westernmost point of land at Ka'ena, beyond paved roads and the last house.

history of police-enforced evictions and the widespread violence that surely would have occurred almost anywhere else.

Sugar employees lived in free company housing at the time; it was the kind of "perquisite" that union members wanted to eliminate in favor of independence and cash. On a subsequent trip to Ewa Plantation, Hall told me a story about company housing that had particularly aggravated the employees, and which emphasized the need to rent and own their own homes. He said company management thought it had satisfied a request for replacement of broken toilet seat covers by installing new seat covers in supervisors' homes and then repainting the used covers for replacement in the housing of union workers. It was not known who in management was responsible for this insensitivity, but union members were outraged. Hall said it was typical of the minor grievances that grew into major issues during the long, difficult strike, which eventually ended with management recognition of the new union and the signing of a contract for full cash wages. It ended the period of indentured laborers and ever-mounting debts at the company store.

At the time, I had been helping organize a downtown Honolulu department store where *haoles* and Orientals working at the same job were paid widely disparate wages. Hall decided it would make a dramatic gesture to have me join the ILWU contract-negotiating committee then in session at the American Factors old office building at the foot of Fort Street. I attended the meeting, and during a particularly tense period, Hall interrupted the company negotiator to introduce me, and to warn his opponent that it might be better to agree on a sugar contract soon, "before Wenkam began to organize the plantation company stores."

It is perhaps illustrative of Hawaii's unusual social environment that, many years later, having in the meantime gone into business for myself as an advertising photographer, American Factors (now Amfac) became one of my best customers, and I was busy producing illustrations for its annual corporate reports. On another occasion, when I encountered opposition in joining the Honolulu Chamber of Commerce because of my "leftist and pro-labor views," as claimed by a chamber officer, I found my entry eased considerably by the new executive director, who said I was just the kind of community activist the chamber needed. The executive director was the retired manager of the department store I had tried to organize many years before.

I served on the Chamber of Commerce's Community Beautification Committee, along with Nancy Bannick, who personally saved many downtown historical buildings before Kukui redevelopment bulldozers flattened everything old; with George Walters, responsible through his landscaping for much of the appearance of Honolulu as we know the city today; and with Alfred Preis, who stopped designing buildings in his own architectural office to help determine the design and appearance of a city growing very rapidly and a bit out of control.

Before the days of environmental activist organizations like the Sierra Club and the Life of the Land, the Chamber of Commerce found itself, through its beautification committee, a strident vocal advocate of environmental preservation, an activity not ordinarily associated with a business-oriented organization. Our primary goal was to change the usual conservationist's "No, no, no" concerning unwanted projects. We developed constructive plans for the advancement of the city's growth in ways that would not harm the island's fragile natural beauty, yet would maintain opportunities for a prosperous business climate.

One of the more lasting ideas dreamed up in our committee was for the creation of an organization of major corporate businesses, with a professional planner at the head, a group that would know everything that was going on in town and would coordinate activities of influential decision-makers. If large corporations were to be making the important investment decisions, we thought they might as well do it on an informed basis and in communication with their peers. The idea thrives today as the Oahu Development Conference, with Aaron Levine as the professional planner.

We originated the proposal for a Nuʻuanu Pali Regional Park, which resulted in banning of restaurant construction at the famed lookout and considerable improvement of public areas. We also wanted Kapiʻolani Park expanded to the sea at Diamond Head. From the chamber's point of view, this translated into quite a controversial proposal when we urged that existing residential lots be rezoned to "parks and open space." They called it "down-zoning;" I called it "up-zoning." And we recommended that the chamber's Board of Directors adopt a resolution opposing construction of any high-rise buildings on the front slopes of Diamond Head. After considerable debate the resolution was approved by one vote. It was probably the first time anywhere a chamber of commerce had voted *not* to build anything!

Probably our most controversial activity was to help push through the Honolulu City Council a restrictive business sign ordinance to keep Oahu from turning into a playground for sign manufacturers. It was evident that most small merchants, and all the large ones, supported our efforts; but a minority threatened to resign from the chamber, feeling it was outrageous for the chamber to be indulging in such "anti-business" activities. Our entire beautification committee was called into a meeting with the membership committee to resolve the problem. They asked us not to ban the signs. We said "no" and continued to work in close collaboration with the Outdoor Circle. The ordinance was duly approved by the city council, but Holiday Inn had to miniaturize their garish logo to conform. McDonald's yellow arches never did appear in Honolulu.

In a year I can't remember now, I was subpoenaed by the Hawaii legislature's Senate-House Un-American Activities Committee. I had previously told the same kind of U.S. congressional committee, then on a junket to Honolulu, that I would be uncooperative and it canceled the subpoena. Now I was to appear at a closed hearing of a local version of political repression, and wasn't too excited over the idea.

The hearing room, on the second floor of the tax collector's building, was somber in color and poorly lighted, with the committee members arrayed evenly along each side of the table with note pads before them, waiting in anticipation for my testimony. The chairman questioned me

---

Agriculture plays a smaller and smaller role all the time. There's very little agriculture. I wouldn't be surprised to see it phase almost completely out — maybe in the next decade. Frankly, I would hate to see it happen, because I think from a visual standpoint it adds an awful lot to the beauty of the island. Just purely from that. But, if this island continues to grow in population you're going to have increasing pressure on that agricultural land which becomes more valuable for homesites.

John Simpson, President
Hawaii Visitors Bureau

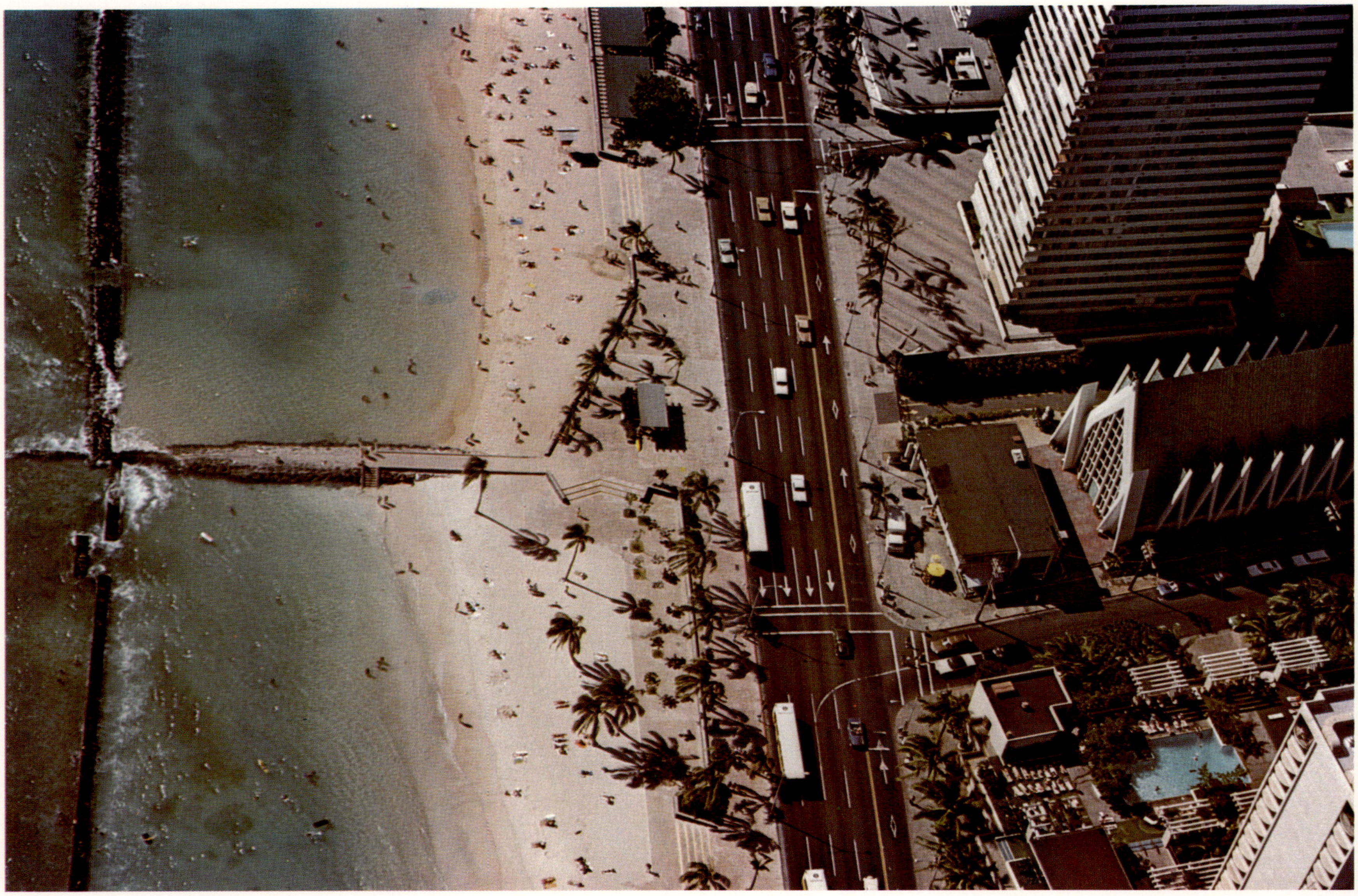

directly and I gave my name, address and telephone number. Then he asked the first germane question, which I expected to be about my labor-organizing activities or friendliness with the ILWU. Instead, he asked quite seriously, "Are you an international Communist spy?"

I was absolutely shocked. I remember at the time thinking that it was a silly question, since if I were a spy I surely wouldn't tell him so. I told the entire committee they could "go to hell," saying I was insulted at the insinuation that I was a foreign spy, and refused to say another word, didn't plead the Fifth Amendment or anything, despite their assertions I would be held in contempt and imprisoned.

I was never jailed and never heard another word from the committee until several years later, at the time of state senate hearings on my confirmation to the state Land Use Commission. The governor's announcement of my appointment had already precipitated an uproar in the conservative community, complaints being made that "a Communist was being added to the governor's cabinet," and that if an environmentalist joined the commission "everyone would soon be living in tents!" Cartoons and editorials, pro and con, appeared in the daily newspapers, and I sat down to listen in on the public hearing with considerable interest.

All the testimony (except for Imua, the local anti-communist group) was in support of my appointment; but most surprising to me were the words of the state senator, now retired, whom I had personally challenged when he was chairman of the state "un-American" committee. He testified that I "was not a Communist, never had been, and would never be one." It was totally unexpected and I thanked him on the way out. In a few days I was confirmed by a majority vote of the state senate. The Democrats voted "yes," the Republicans voted "no," but then I was never much of a Republican.

Almost exactly one month after the voting in my first Land Use Commission meeting, the same senator telephoned me for a private appointment at my office. I should never have wondered, in my naive way, what was wanted. He brought a large map, which he unrolled on my desk, to locate the property of a client of his, pointing out how the conservation district boundaries seemed to encroach upon the adjacent land parcel. He asked if I didn't agree that all of his client's property shouldn't be zoned urban. "It was probably a mistake, wasn't it?" It was my first encounter with the wondrous convolutions of American democracy. In some ways, I guess, Hawaii politics are the same as everywhere else.

My years on the commission were constructive and eventful. I learned the basic principles of legislative democracy — how to trade votes — and was able personally to investigate stories told of political commissioners who are invited to elaborate dinner parties, complete with all you want to drink and girls for the evening — it's true. I think every developer and landowner in the state bought me a drink at one time or another. It was difficult to sit down at a hotel bar and pay my own check. Someone across the room always paid it first. It was, in a way, disappointing to me that no conservationist ever bought me dinner or a drink. A free drink never influenced my vote, but the friendships that developed were lopsided when they were all landowners. However, the lobbying didn't change my environmental goals, for after three and a half years on the commission, the acreage of conservation-zoned land had almost doubled.

When my first term on the commission expired, Governor Burns reappointed me for another, also requiring confirmation by the senate. Three days before senate adjournment, with no appearance on the senate floor of an appropriate resolution for my confirmation, I inquired among my legislator friends about what was happening. They informed me it probably was in the senate president's desk drawer. I asked the senator and he said it would stay there, and if I wanted it out to go ask my ILWU friends. I did, and they said I wasn't "playing the game properly." My name never came to a vote in the senate, where it undoubtedly would have received approval. I later learned that two subdivisions planned for agricultural and conservation land, which would require rezoning to urban, were never built because of my vote against them. Both projects were supported by the senate president and the clerk of the senate. It was apparent I had done my job too well. ■

What balance between good and evil our civilized ways will bring, we cannot now foretell; but experience shows that they destroy unprotected wilderness and wildlife with appalling ruthlessness; and that, unlike man's civilizations, destroyed nature cannot be rebuilt. Once violated it is gone forever, as is the ancient beauty of Waikiki beach.

Charles A. Lindbergh
Conservationist

Kuhio Beach, Kalakaua Boulevard, and St. Catherine's Church, Waikiki.

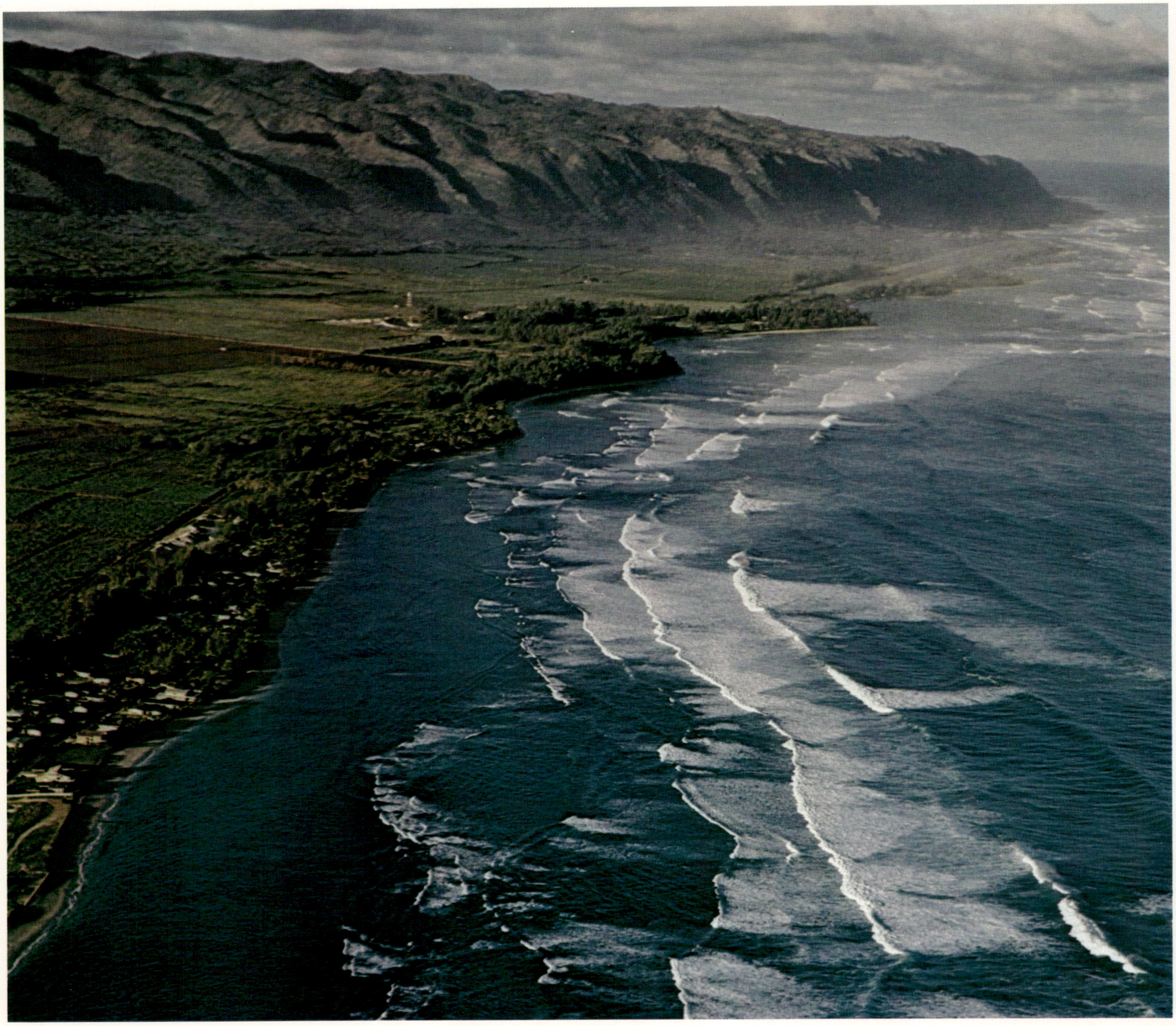

The Surf Is Up

Hawaiians were great navigators of the open sea, possessing considerable knowledge of wave patterns and currents, of the harmony and rhythm of wave sets, storm waves, and wind waves. Like so much in the Hawaiian lifestyle that is close to nature, riding these waves on a board and body surfing on the giant waves that broke upon the coral sand must have been the quintessential acts of an island people.

They were very much at home on the sea and spoke knowingly of the ocean in words that have no English equivalent. There are different words for the three waves in a set: *kakala* is the first "roller;" *pakaiea*, the second set; and *opu'u*, the third. Where the waves actually break, is *po'inakai*. *Kai-kohala* is the shoal water extending shoreward ahead of moving waves, indicative of good surfing conditions.

Hawaiians rode the first heavy *koa* planks on their bellies, in time developing the techniques of standing upon and maneuvering a board in the surf. Sacred grounds were dedicated to surfing, and special chants spoken to call up the surf and announce contests, which often lasted several days, providing personal enjoyment and testing of physical skills.

The sport virtually disappeared in the years after Captain Cook, when Hawaiian chiefs changed the islands from a subsistence economy to a money system. Commoners were taxed heavily in order to obtain goods to trade with foreigners. Complete families were sent into the mountains for sandalwood. Little time remained for water sports.

In the old days surfers were always nude, and when a man and woman found themselves riding the same long wave together they generally celebrated the ride upon reaching shore — making love on the sand, just beyond the sweep of the highest wave. The missionaries soon forbade the sport completely, and ancient skills were nearly nonexistent for over a hundred years until surfing experienced a revival in the early part of this century.

As old skills were sharpened, the heavy ten-foot wood boards with square tails became hollow, lighter, and shorter. Fiberglass and foam allowed new freedom of design, and boards were custom-built for wave height, surfer's weight, and surfing style. Young Californians helped rediscover the old surfing grounds, unused by tourists, on the west and north shores of Oahu, and they rapidly changed the sport from riding waves "just for fun" into the competitive events of old Hawaiian times. The Duke Kahanamoku Surfing Classic became an international event, first on the waves at Makaha in Waianae, then in later years on the "big ones" — tube riding at off-the-wall and Sunset Beach. Those were the days of "endless summer," and a new surfing vocabulary — off-the-lip, pipeline, velzyland — the years when Hawaiian waves gained their reputation of having a "punch" like no others.

Surfers now talk of "radical aggression" and "clear-flowing" styles, the ascetics of surfing differing greatly from old Hawaiian attitudes. The sport of Hawaiian *ali'i* has spawned a new generation of fanatical devotees enveloped in a philosophy of life responsive only to the unrequited joy of riding a wave. Their entire experience is the personification of being free, with an accompanying social life that allows it.

The fleet of battered vans and bugs with board racks cluster along north shore beaches like ants at a picnic, their brown occupants watching the tide and counting sets, their women clustered behind and slightly to one side. Should the sea flatten or the afternoon winds ruffle the waves, the entourage will move on to check out other more promising reef systems, where hidden undersea contours may still produce a curl on the foaming crest and a tube to ride out of.

In ancient days the Sunset Beach surf was called Paumalu after the adjacent *ahupua'a*, and even in those times the waves had a reputation among *ali'i* as a fierce surf. When Chief Kahikilani of Kauai came to Oahu to surf, he was riding the giant waves at Paumalu when the legendary Bird Maiden saw him and immediately fell in love. She sent her messengers to give him an orange *lehua lei* and guide him to her cave, where he was considerably enamoured by her love. The chief stayed for many days until he heard the high surf one day and longed to ride the waves again.

The Bird Maiden allowed him to return to the surf if he vowed never to kiss another woman; but after surfing all day, he made love to a beautiful Oahu girl who rode together with him on the last wave and then placed an *'ilima lei* around his neck. The Bird Maiden's messengers saw Kahikilani break his vow, and told her what had happened. When she realized Kahikilani would never return, she turned him into stone and as a rock he remains today — on the hill above Sunset, watching the high surf at Paumalu. ■

Along the Mokule'ia shore, high seas generated by a northern Pacific storm reach Oahu. The surf is up at "Avalanche".

High surf curls across the fringing reef at Paʻumalu (Sunset Beach).

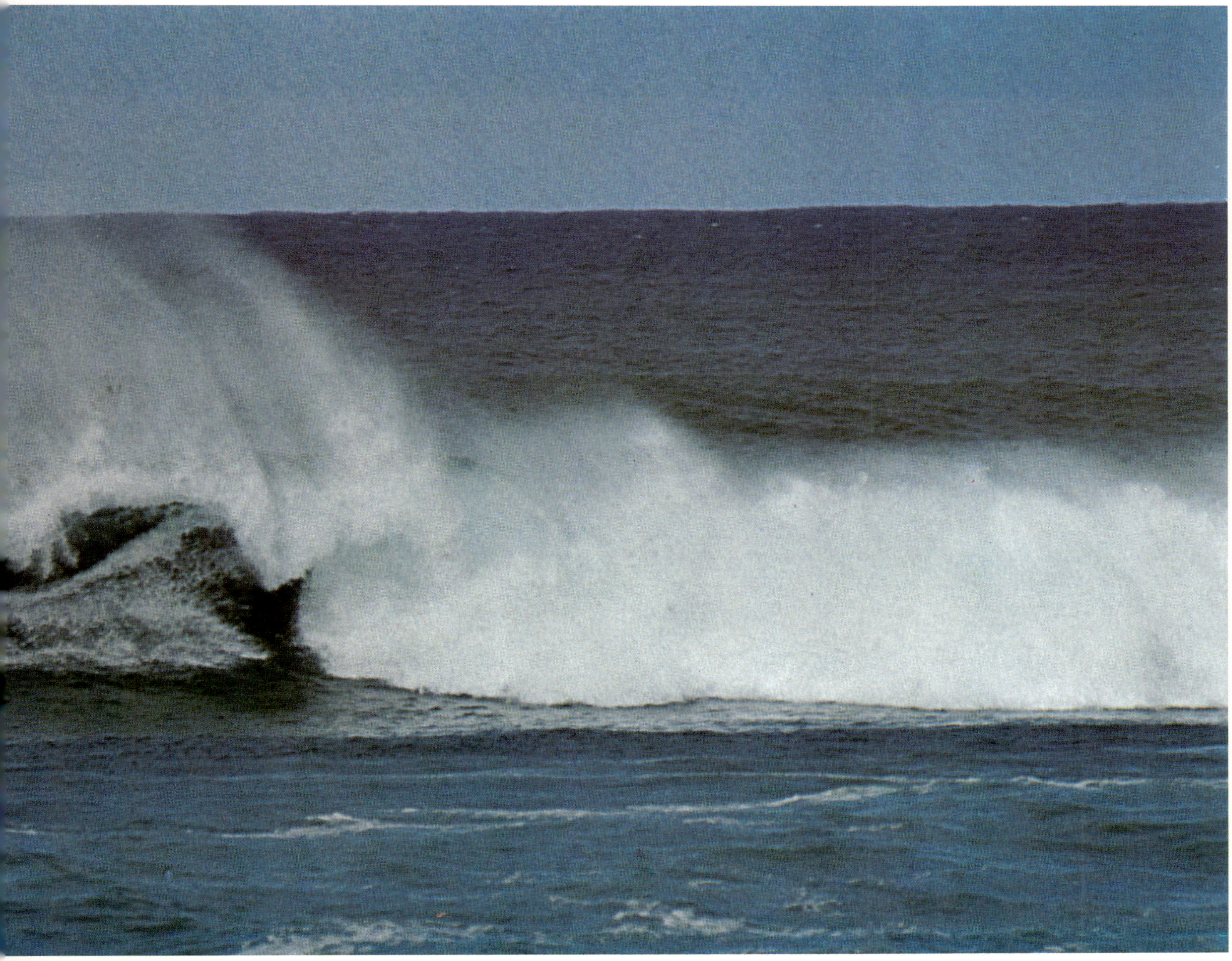

Hiram Fong — Chinn Ho — John Burns — Dan Inouye — Elmer Cravalho
Riley Allen — Henry Kaiser — Duke Kahanamoku — Oren Long — Walter Dillingham
Jack Hall — Joe Farrington — Sanford Dole
Capt. Cook — Liliuokalani — Kamehameha IV — Father Damien
Kamehameha I — Prince Kuhio — Charles Bishop — Bernice Pauahi — Queen Emma

The People Who Made It So

The city of Honolulu was too young to celebrate America's Bicentennial. Captain Cook had not yet discovered the Sandwich Islands (as he called them) for the British Crown at the time when Massachusetts minutemen returned the fire of British troops on Bunker Hill. Nor had the missionaries yet been ordained. Kamehameha was still a young warrior fighting with spears; his establishment of the kindom of Hawaii, after conquering the islands one by one, was an achievement still many years in the future.

Cook's flagship, the *Resolution,* was a refitted coal collier restored to service for his third voyage by a British admiralty with few available ships. King George III's newest vessels were being used to send replacement troops for the British armies in New England. In a letter to friends written prior to sailing, Cook lamented over the ill-advised British military intervention in the New World that deprived him of new vessels for what he considered the greater priority of Pacific exploration. Even the revolutionary American government considered Cook's Pacific voyages of great importance, for when the British government asked Ben Franklin, then American Commissioner to France, to provide safe passage for Cook on his return to England, it was promptly granted by American authorities. Cook was unable to avail himself of this courtesy, however, because he died in Hawaii on the shores of Kealakekua Bay.

Hawaii was possibly the last place on earth to be discovered and settled when the Polynesians opted for a change in political climate and sailed north, reaching landfall on the Big Island's South Cape only 700 years ago. Cook followed 500 years later, navigating with sailing instructions provided by the king of Tahiti and a well-informed local sailor named Tupaea, who had helped him explore nearby islands and undoubtedly told him about Hawaii. The two British ships sailed straight north to Hawaii with only one stop, over the holidays, at Christmas Island to replenish stores of water and fresh food. Cook appeared to know exactly where he was going.

Boston missionaries sailed to Hawaii years later by request of disgruntled Hawaiian commoners appalled at the continuing fighting between chiefs and a cruel *kapu* system that enforced the death penalty for anyone allowing his shadow to fall upon the *ali'i*. However, the archaic Hawaii *kapu* system and idol worship were abolished by the Hawaiians themselves before missionaries arrived to prepare the islands' political, moral, and economic environment for later planters and merchants.

The people who made a significant impact on the islands, and who determined the direction that Hawaii would move among nations, are relatively few in number and it is not difficult for historians to follow the trail of growth and development of the Hawaiian kingdom, republic, territory, and state — all occurring in less than 200 years, within the life span of the United States.

Much of what has occurred in Hawaii has been a

Hawaiian Independent Refinery, Inc., Campbell Industrial Park.

Twenty-two men and women selected by editors of the *Honolulu Star-Bulletin* as people of lasting significance in the history of Hawaii. Some are living legends, most are gone and still controversial, all have left their personal imprint on Honolulu, home of kings, site of the only royal palace in the U.S., and capital of Hawaii since 1893. Drawings by Ray Higuchi.

"palace revolution." Only in recent years has the general population become involved in the decision making process. A strong middle class, with influence at all levels of society — economic, social, and political — did not exist to any significant extent until post-World War II events forced major changes in the plantation system and mainland investors were able to enter the Hawaii market. Kresge and Sears were first to break the local merchants' monopoly before the war. Following union organization of sugar and pineapple plantations by Jack Hall and the longshoremen's union (ILWU), economic pressures were effectively combined with political action to create a new Democratic party. Joined in collaboration with young Japanese-Americans returning from the war, Hawaii changed rapidly into a democratic, sophisticated community.

Many people were involved in this growth and development; but over the seven centuries of Hawaii's short history, only a few individuals assumed leadership roles and were responsible for a significant impact on the economic and political life of Hawaii. It is these few who took the necessary bold steps, often facing considerable adversity, but always with subjective knowledge of the correct time to act, to move forward — a little ahead of when the people themselves were ready to accept changes begun in the best interest of Hawaii's future.

A list of these history makers, compiled by the editors of the *Honolulu Star-Bulletin,* is an excellent introduction to the history of Hawaii and Honolulu.

Senator Hiram Fong, first Republican U.S. senator from Hawaii, financier.
Captain James Cook, British explorer.
Chinn Ho, financier, developer of Ilikai and Makaha.
Governor John Burns, founder new Democratic Party of Hawaii, delegate to Congress during statehood campaign, second elected governor of Hawaii.
Father Damien, priest to the Molokai lepers.
Senator Dan Inuoye, U.S. Democrat senator, first U.S. Democrat representative from Hawaii.
Charles Bishop, sugar planter, royal minister.
Mayor Elmer Cravalho, Maui County, state Speaker of the House.
Riley Allen, editor *Honolulu Star-Bulletin.*
Henry Kaiser, industrialist, developer of Kaiser Hawaiian Village Hotel and Hawaii Kai.
Jack Hall, regional director of ILWU, union organizer.
Duke Kahanamoku, gold medal in Olympic swimming, father of modern surfing.
Prince Jonah Kuhio Kalanianaole, ten-term delegate to Congress, initiator of Hawaiian Homes Commission.
Senator Oren Long, territorial governor, first Democrat U.S. senator from Hawaii.
Walter Dillingham, organized Hawaiian Dredging Company, built first Pearl Harbor drydock and harbors throughout Hawaii.
King Kamehameha IV and his wife, Queen Emma, established schools and founded Queen's Hospital; royal palace given one of his Hawaiian names, 'Iolani.
Joe Farrington, newspaper publisher, delegate to congress at time of first moves for statehood.
President Sanford Dole, Republic of Hawaii, first governor of territory of Hawaii.
King Kamehameha I, conqueror of the islands, founder of the kingdom of Hawaii.
Queen Liliuokalani, last royal ruler, composer, "Aloha Oe."
Princess Bernice Pauahi Bishop, founder of the Bishop Estate and Kamehameha School, last of the Kamehamehas.

Two women who should be added to the list are Chieftess Kapi'olani, who successfully challenged the wrath of Pele, the volcano goddess, on the edge of erupting Halema'uma'u firepit, and Ka'ahumanu, the *kuhina nui,* who first advocated eating with men. Ka'ahumanu, the favorite wife of Kamehameha I, whose rule was something like a police state, decided before his death in 1819 that the *kapu* system must be abolished. She may have begun the women's movement in Hawaii over 150 years ago.

Not eating certain foods, according to Hawaiian historian Kamakau, was "a profound act of submission to the will of the gods." It was believed that for men and women to eat together was disrespectful. Ka'ahumanu was particularly anxious to break the eating *kapu* and enjoy pig and bananas along with the men, but she waited until the mourning period was over for Kamehameha I, before arranging a sit-down dinner with the men.

It apparently was quite an event, according to oral chroniclers of the time. The new king, Liholiho, was invited, but for two days he and his chiefs waited offshore of the dinner site in Kailua, drinking rum aboard his two-masted canoes. When the wind died down and the king's canoe was becalmed, Ka'ahumanu sent a double canoe to tow the reluctant monarch ashore for dinner. On this first night he ate some dog that had been previously available only to chieftesses, and several times entered the once-forbidden women's *lau hala* house. Men drank rum with women and smoked tobacco together. Those

Descendents of the varied people who made history in Honolulu visit King Kamehameha's *lei* shrouded memorial on his birthday celebration. Black gowned descendents of Hawaiian *ali'i*, trimmed with orange ilima flowers join an elderly Japanese-American representative of early plantation immigrants, contemporary young city women, and the ever-present mainland visitor—standing slightly apart and perhaps not fully understanding the significance of this unusual gathering of people in downtown Honolulu. Overleaf is the magnificent bowl of Hanauma Bay Beach Park on Oahu's south shore, site of the first underwater marine preserve in the nation.

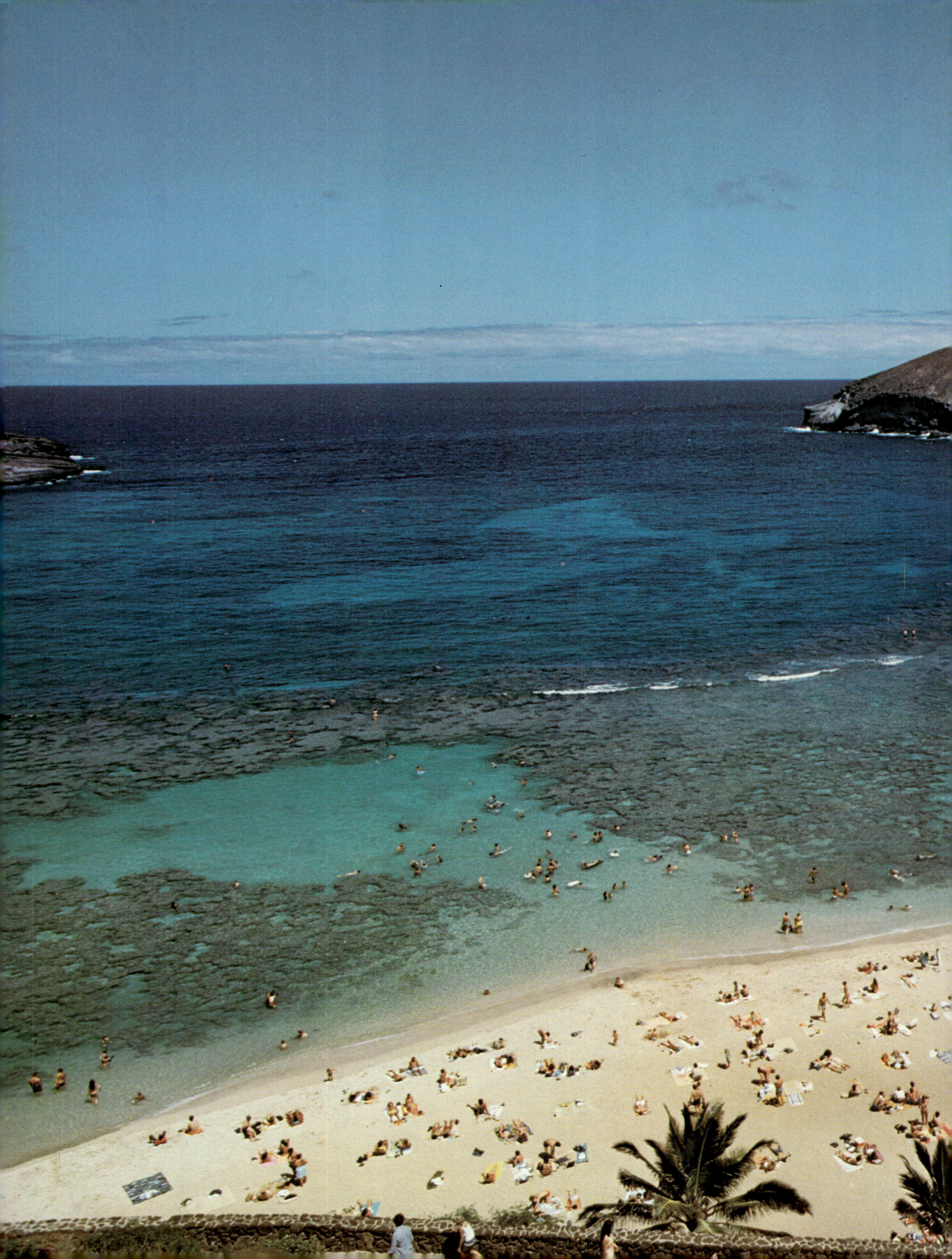

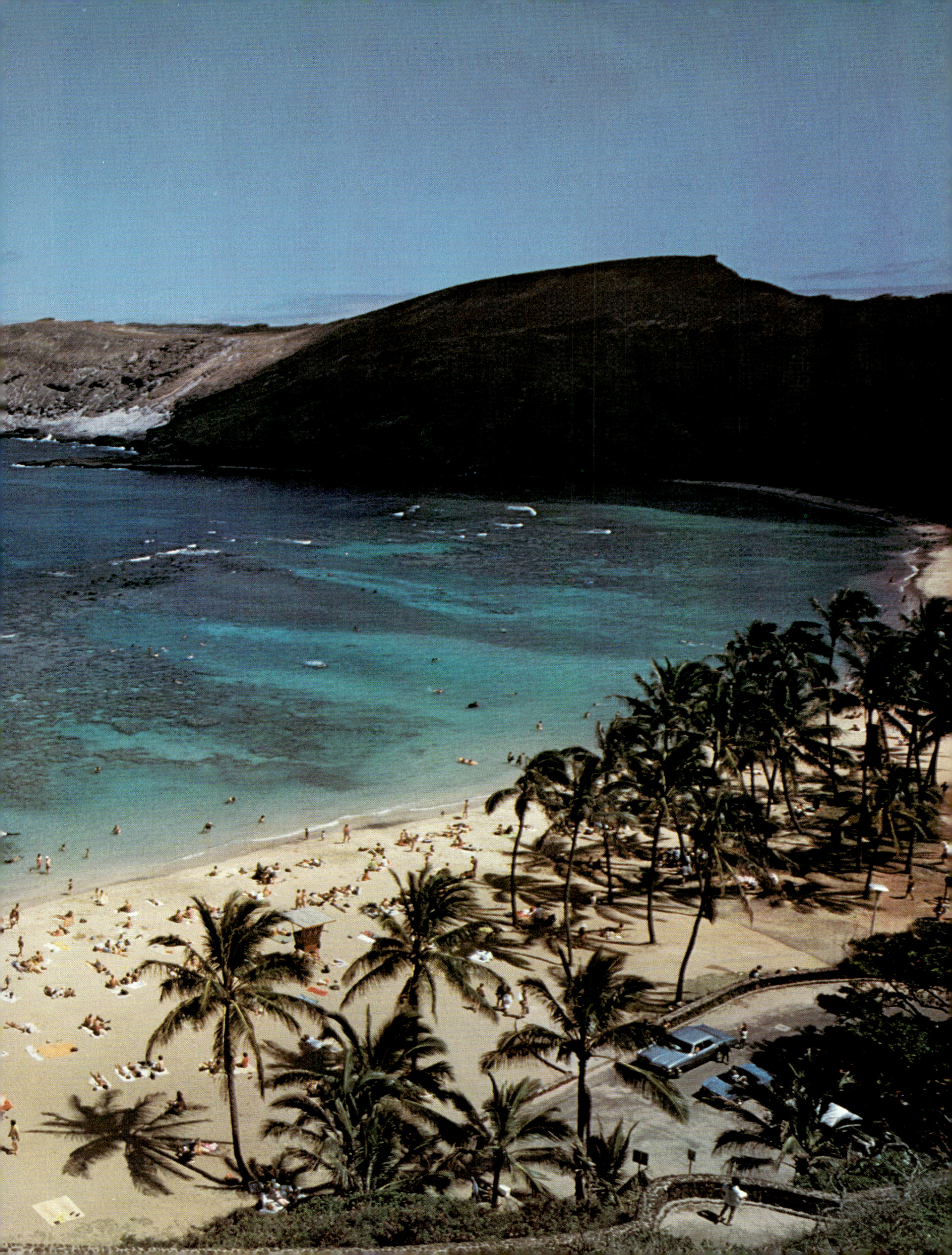

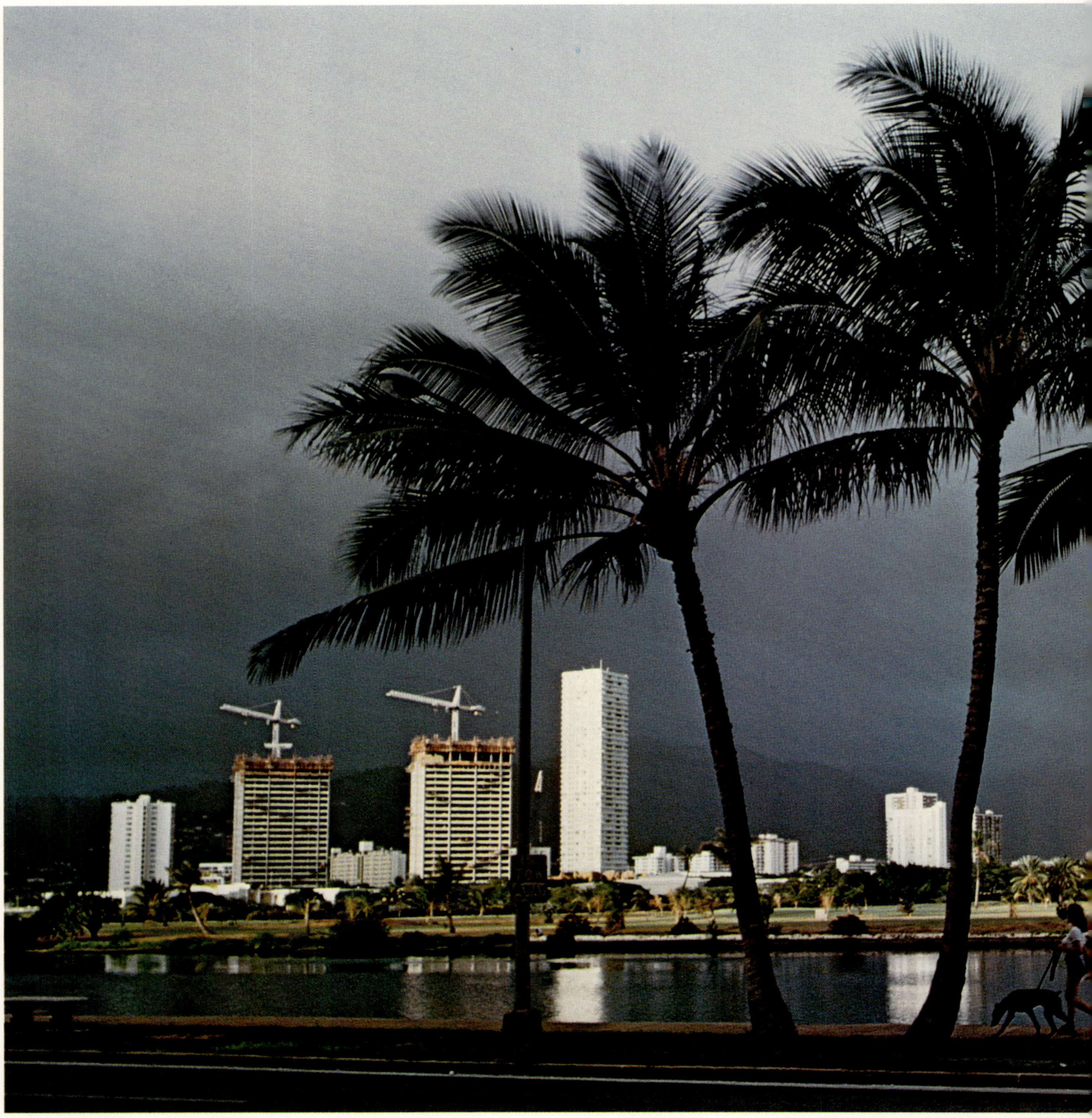

Construction cranes, the "native bird" of the construction industry, raises condominiums to house Honolulu's slowly increasing population. They embellish the skyline dramatically along the Ala Wai Canal, dredged to drain the original swamps of Waikiki.

watching are said to have shouted, "The tabus are at an end! The gods are a lie!" Kaʻahumanu asked the king to "make eating free over the whole kingdom from Hawaii to Oahu," and it was done. Sacred images were burned, *heiau* torn down, and great feasts of *kapu*-free eating were enjoyed throughout the islands.

Under Kamehameha III, Honolulu became the capital city, with elaborate balls given by the king, who issued invitations printed on white satin. Operas and concerts were in vogue. And Hawaiian royalty traveled abroad to be received and entertained by the crowned heads of Europe.

While there was some interest by imperial powers in colonizing Hawaii, nothing of consequence happened until American sugar planters and merchants recognized the favorable business opportunities and began to agitate for annexation by the U.S. Once in 1843 the British flag flew over Honolulu, but five months later Queen Victoria sent word to Kamehameha III that it was a mistake. Upon raising the Hawaiian flag again, the king in appreciation said: *Ua mau ke ea o ka aina i ka pono* (The life of the land is perpetuated by righteousness). His words became the motto of Hawaii.

These, then, are the people who have made the difference. Others might also be included if we knew who they were. Some have been forgotten as new leaders followed with new accomplishments. Still more have never been recognized for their contributions, or their names were erased by a displeased establishment.

In years to come the list will surely include leaders in the tourist industry and even environmentalists, when we are able, in the light of history, to measure their special impact. I know that I would want to include the woman who first said we should have no billboards in Hawaii and decided to do something about it — and eventually did succeed in having them banned. There is Lorrin Thurston, who over considerable opposition pushed on until Congress approved establishment of Hawaii National Park (now divided into two great parks, Hawaii Volcanoes National Park and Haleakala National Park). Perhaps some would want to rate highly the very important skills of legislator and lawyer Tom Gill, who obtained the vital information necessary to stop construction of the proposed double-deck "interstate" freeway along Ala Moana. Gill was also a prime mover in pushing Hawaii's controversial land use law through the state legislature. He called it the "greenbelt" law to make the package more acceptable for opponents.

Two commoners, a missionary-educated Hawaiian scholar, and a mainland *haole* who settled in Honolulu in 1847, also warrant listing: Samuel Manaiakalani Kamakau, a graduate of Lahainaluna School, an active politician, and a prolific writer of Hawaiian history; and Abraham Fornander, who married a Hawaiian chiefess from Molokai, worked as a newspaper editor, and ultimately became a justice of the Hawaii Supreme Court.

Both of these men became proficient in the written Hawaiian language evolved by missionaries and were first to translate the oral history of Hawaii as passed down through the ages in chants and *mele*. Our appreciation of Hawaiian traditions and lore is possible because of their published work. The fragments of song, dance, mythology, and Polynesian lifestyle that have gradually become part of our own contemporary island lore, are the unusual benefits derived from Kamakau and Fornander, who transformed "legendary" chants and geneology into written history. Because of them we can better appreciate and adapt the unique gifts of Polynesia.

Aristotle wrote that, "Men come together in the city to live; they remain there in order to live the good life." Honolulu is the kind of city where many influential men and women have gathered together and stayed to enrich each other and future generations. The history of Hawaii must be why Honolulu is the place to live the good life. ■

I went up to Oakland to train to fight professional. It was all right, but not like Hawaii. You know, people not as friendly over there as they are here. Like there, if you get sick, if you're in your house, you don't even know your neighbor. They don't even bother with you. You could be dead in your house for all they know, and they wouldn't even find you maybe for one or two weeks. Honolulu everybody help each other. If your neighbors need help, well, you help them. You have a kind of ohana *feeling.*

Gilbert Rivera
Driver for "da Bus"

Ohiʻalehua blossoms in her hair. Lehua was the name given to the first warrior killed in battle.

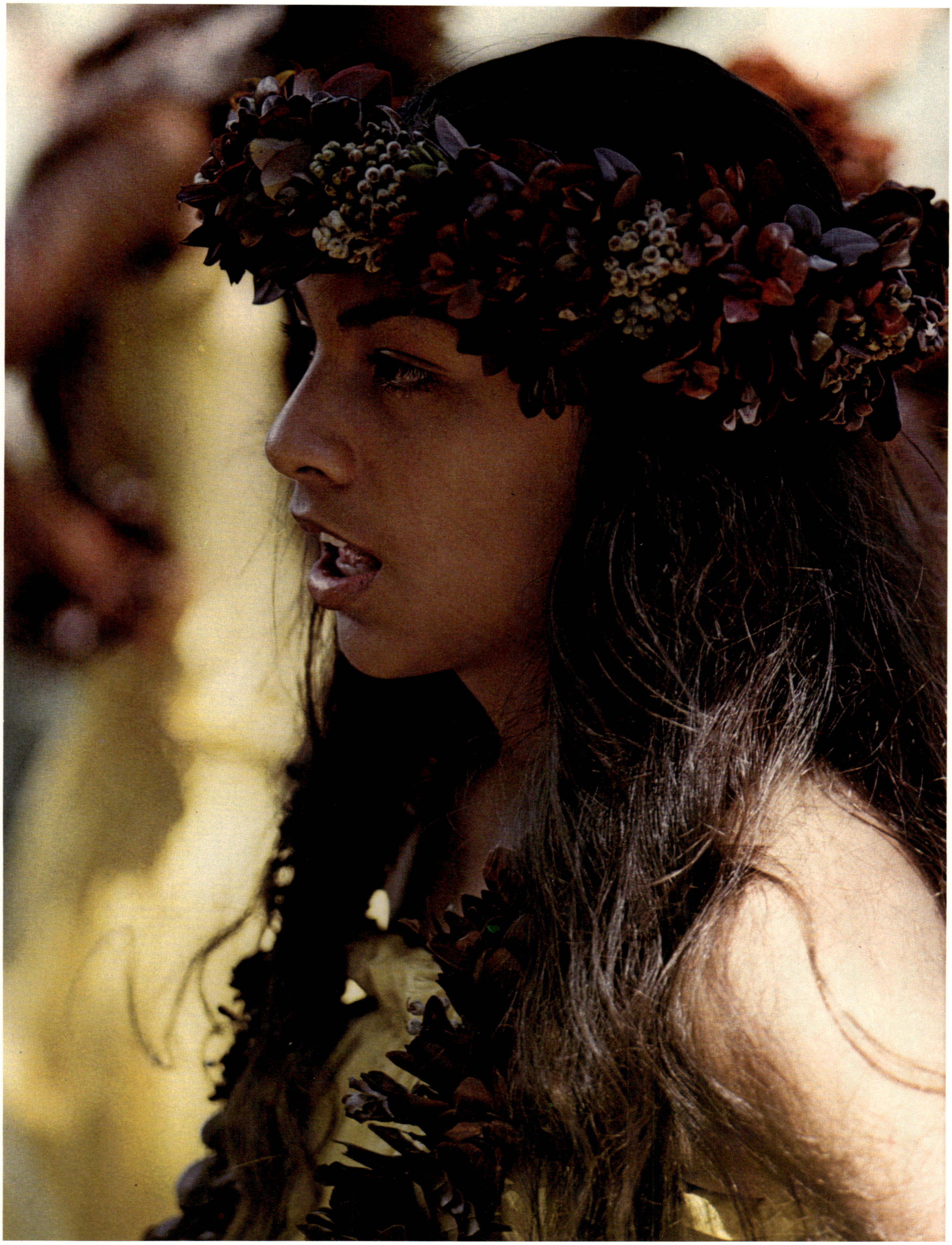

Only In Honolulu

Several years passed before it was finally agreed whether the city or the state would clean up the seaweed covering Waikiki Beach after Kona storms. (The city). It still has not been definitely confirmed if it is legal for city lifeguards to work from state-controlled beach lands to rescue out-of-state tourists. Continuing jurisdictional struggles between the city and state had caused state grass-mowing crews to stop clearing weeds from city bridge approaches, until someone reasoned that when 82 percent of the state's population lives in one city, everyone using the highway must be from the same place. Many of us have also wondered where city streets become state roads and federal aid highways begin. We still call highways by name rather than by the arbitrary numbers that come with federal highway funds, and it has always been a mystery how Senator Dan Inouye was able to have Hawaii included as part of the interstate highway system, when Hawaii is 2,400 miles from the nearest state! It is matters of this import that keep any really clear analysis of Honolulu at arms length.

This is the place where a bumper sticker says "Honk if you Hula," where Sears offers a "mildew wash" service — possibly the only mildew removal specialists in the world — and where national TV advertising for antifreeze is totally wasted. In the Hawaii legislature a few years back, Senator Kazuhisa Abe actually introduced a bill abolishing Christmas after his fellow legislators stubbornly refused to declare Buddha's birthday a state holiday. Christmas won.

Meanwhile at City Hall, Councilman George "Scotty" Koga voiced his displeasure at the food dished up by Ala Moana Park concessionaires. "I wish they would improve the quality of their hot dogs. I was very, very disappointed," he said at a meeting of the council's Finance Committee. City business stopped while the size and price of hot dogs was considered before taking action on a resolution making the semiautonomous Honolulu Board of Water Supply a regular city department. The committee needed a performance audit of the water board.

The water board manager and chief engineer, Edward Hirata, gulped, then tried to explain why in the two months since the water board was trying to get everyone in Hawaii to reduce water use by 10 percent, the water board's own consumption climbed 14 percent. The water people increased their consumption by one and a half million gallons more in one month. Hirata explained that a new reservoir in Kuilima was landscaped and considerable irrigation was required. Then two other reservoirs in

Polynesian Cultural Center, La'ie.

For business, I like the growth, naturally, being a food broker. It's good for my business. I can sell the tourist hotels, restaurants, but I think personally I don't like the growth. I like it better the way it was in the old days. Where everything was open and you could go to the beach when you wanted to and you weren't afraid to walk out into the streets. I don't like the one-way streets, but this is progress. When you have the amount of tourists you have in Waikiki it does get to be a jungle.

Clifford Kramer
Meat broker, Kailua

Aiea were very leaky, accounting for a million gallons down the drain — and they were still trying to find out how the missing water leaked out of a St. Louis Heights tank. Hirata hoped "the public has enough confidence in our overall program so they won't let temporary problems cloud the issue." It was fortunate the council's performance audit request was delayed by the hot dogs at Ala Moana.

Then the garbage department had a serious problem to contend with over Christmas. It seems the trash collectors were concerned about the occasional cases of Primo beer left out for them by friendly residents. Would these gifts represent a violation of the code of ethics? It all depends. If the beer was intended to keep the trash collectors from roughing up their garbage cans, it was probably extortion or outright bribery, according to some legal briefs. The board of ethics will probably meet in executive session to provide an advisory opinion.

Following the victory of a new city law prohibiting dogs from barking, the Citizens Against Noise announced a new noise target: tour buses. "We can't afford to let tourism's noise problems generate hostility among residents," said William J. Atkinson, the organization's noise problems' committee chairman. He added, "When motors are left running to keep air conditioning going next to apartment buildings while tourists visit a park, have a meal, see a show; or when quiet residential streets become noisy so tour buses can avoid a traffic light, the 'aloha spirit' wears thin."

Citizens Against Noise proposed that the city council set up another task force just like it did to quiet the dogs. In the meantime, Mayor Frank Fasi signed the dog ordinance into law, providing a fine of up to $50 and a possible jail term of up to 30 days for the owner of a dog that barks too long or too loudly. Previously passed laws kept dogs on a leash and picked up after; now it is illegal to bark incessantly for 10 minutes or intermittently for 30.

At a public hearing prior to the law's passage, the Hawaiian Humane Society advised dog owners having difficulty with dogs barking to call the dog's name, shout "No," and douse it with water. One distressed owner replied that his dog is pedigreed and all pedigreed dogs are named Titcomb's Alfred Prince Snowfield of Sandringham Greystones, and "By the time I finished shouting Titcomb's Alfred Prince Snowfield of Sandringham Greystones, no!, the dog figured out he was going to get doused and he was halfway to Waimanalo — barking."

Each year, Bob Krauss, columnist for the *Honolulu Advertiser*, reviews the new telephone directory to uncover any important trends that may be underway. In the latest directory he noted that the "Smiths have overtaken the Chuns as Honolulu's fifth biggest family and pizza has swept past chop suey in the Yellow Pages."

Krauss considers the latest directory exciting but difficult to interpret, noting, "There's something stirring in there but I'm not sure what it is." As long as he can remember, chop suey has been undisputed champion of foods advertised in the yellow pages with around 3 pages. There are 3¼ pages of chop suey currently, a slight increase. But pizza has jumped from 2 pages to 4¼ in an unprecedented history-making shift in Honolulu taste or in number of fast food outlets. Hawaiian *luaus* have held steady at less than a page.

As far as ethnic groups are concerned, the conglomerate Lees (Chinese or Korean or Caucasian) continue to lead all other Honolulu families with 19 columns, closely followed by 17¼ columns of Wong numbers. Then come the Youngs (12 columns) and the Changs (11¼ columns).

Since Krauss began reviewing the telephone directory in the 1960s, the Changs and the Chuns have been in either fourth or fifth place in alternate years. This year the Smiths (who must like pizza) have overtaken the Chuns, 10¼ to 10 columns for fifth place. This drops the faltering Chuns, according to Krauss's research, to sixth place. Next comes the Chings (9½ columns), then the Nakamuras (9 columns), the Lums (8 columns) and the Yamamotos (only 7 columns). The Tanakas (6½ columns) dropped out of the top 10 and, as possibly indicative of the new Hawaiian society, the Browns, Millers, and

---

Well, I was born here, you see, and I'm going to spend the rest of my life here, so I guess that speaks enough for it. Honolulu is not, naturally, what it was fifty years ago or even longer. But that's progress, and I think comparing the old to the new is crazy, because there is nothing to be gained with comparing the old with the new. They say the old Honolulu didn't have the night clubs — something going on every night. Well, we didn't want it that way. Some of us don't even care for it now, but it's there to be taken for what it's worth.

Vernon "Red" McQueen
Sports writer

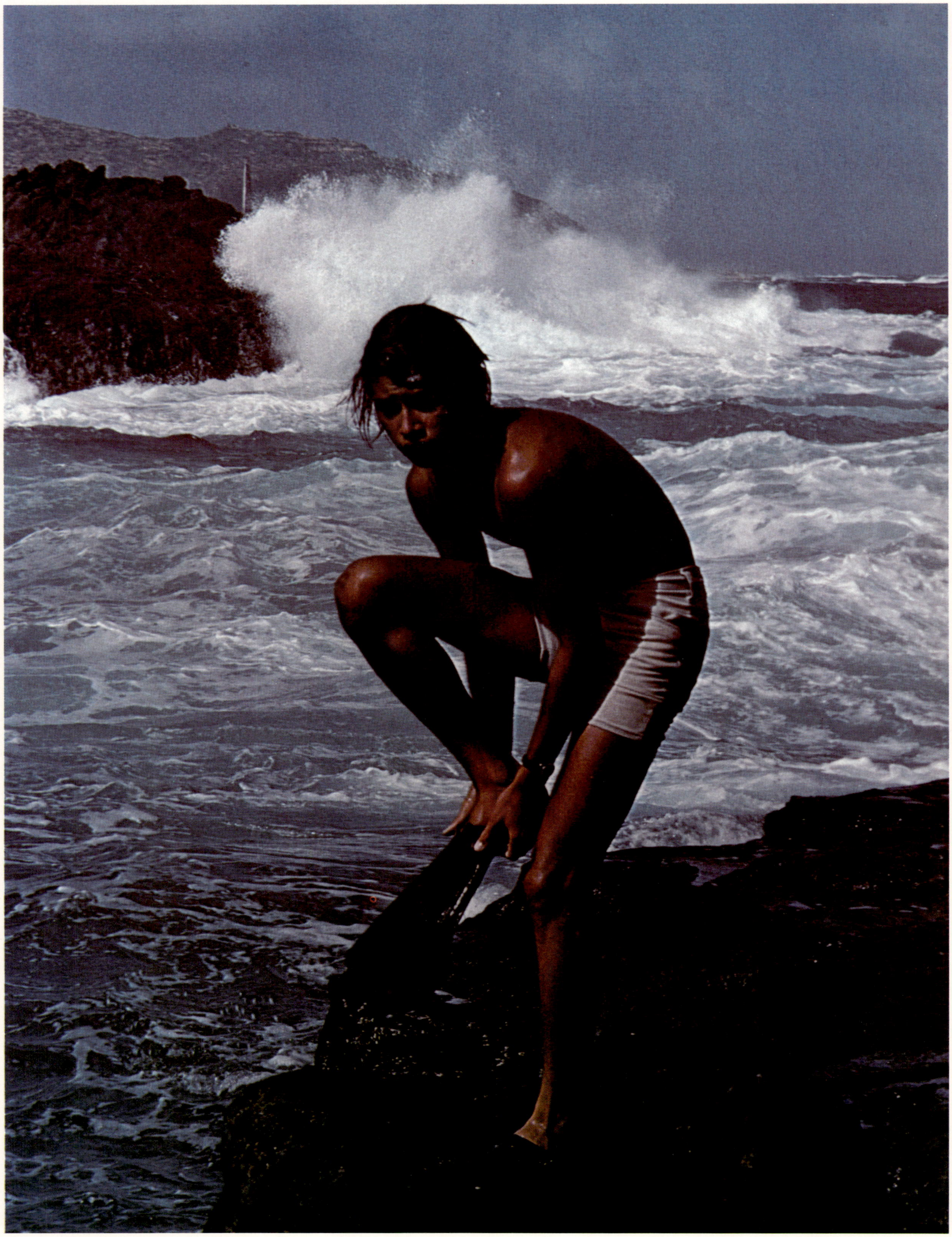

Williamses are now creeping into position to offer a challenge.

Then there was the great canoe snafu when the Outrigger Canoe Club won a 37-minute victory over the Tahitian team in the annual Molokai-to-Oahu canoe race during Aloha Week. Teiki Tamari, a paddler for the Tahitians, wanted a rematch because the Hawaii canoe, "Manu' Ula," he said, didn't meet Hawaiian design specifications — it was of Tahitian design and made of fiberglass. The Tahitians had won the year before in a Tahitian design made of wood.

And Leslie Okumura was absent from part of his trial because he was receiving treatment for a broken arm suffered while trying to escape the courthouse where he was being tried for escaping from Oahu Prison (where so many prisoners were escaping at one time that pundits suggested posting a sign for the street — "Danger, prisoners escaping"). He missed closing arguments and return of the guilty verdict, so the Hawaii Supreme Court reversed his conviction, saying the defendant wasn't present during part of the trial and ordered a new one.

Ocean waters between the islands making up Honolulu and the state are, by federal court decision, international waters, making the short 30-minute trip to Molokai Island an international excursion. Local airlines are not flying intrastate, but operate under CAB regulations like national carriers. Only recently enacted laws reserving fishing and resource rights within 200 miles around the islands limit foreign mining on the Molokai shoals. In past years elements of the Soviet's Pacific Fleet regularly cruised a zigzag route through the island chain, testing their right to sail in the international waters of Honolulu.

Honolulu politics, like most small-town politics, presents many twists and turns, mostly revolving around various personalities rather than political parties, and all of the involved machinations are of a kind that is very difficult if not impossible to describe to an outsider. Possibly the best way to offer an introduction to Honolulu politics is to provide a brief commentary on the most intriguing local political affair in recent years, an elaborate confrontation involving the governor and mayor: the Kukui Plaza Caper. This was a political redevelopment farce in many acts and with a surprise ending, taking place mostly in the Honlulu City Council chambers because everyone else in City Hall denied that anything took place.

Sources close to the Kukui Plaza affair said it was remarkably successful at its apparent purpose — to provide gainful employment for witnesses, jurors, reporters, lawyers, guards, city councilmen, and one lawyer from Los Angeles. The *Honolulu Advertiser* quoted a usually reliable source after proceedings had been underway for a year, that it might go on forever, and that the hearings and trial were "thought to be the fourth or fifth biggest industry in Hawaii." One economist, who asked not to be identified, said, "We ought to be thankful it will never end. If it ever did, the number of people thrown out of work could trigger a depression." It is estimated that participants on both sides spent over one million dollars on the event.

The council had been feuding with the mayor for some time, so the members took this opportunity to begin a public investigation of Kukui and the mayor. Using subpoenas combined with considerable fanfare and press conferences, they began by picking as chairman of their investigating committee a councilman who switched from Democrat to Republican to run against Fasi for mayor, an

Cartoon by Corky Trinidad, courtesy *Honolulu Star-Bulletin*.

Rough seas are no deterrent to a young Hawaiian swimmer at the Blowhole along Oahu's south shore.

Waikiki skyline, 1941.

Waikiki skyline, 1955.

Waikiki skyline, 1978.

Honolulu is a changing city in many ways, and the visual changes are dramatically revealed in the continuously changing skyline of Waikiki, built alongside the unchanging ocean, against the lower mountain slopes and craters, and below the trade wind clouds, all providing the natural environment for an island city. Overleaf is Waikiki from the air, the nation's most famous and most desired vacation destination.

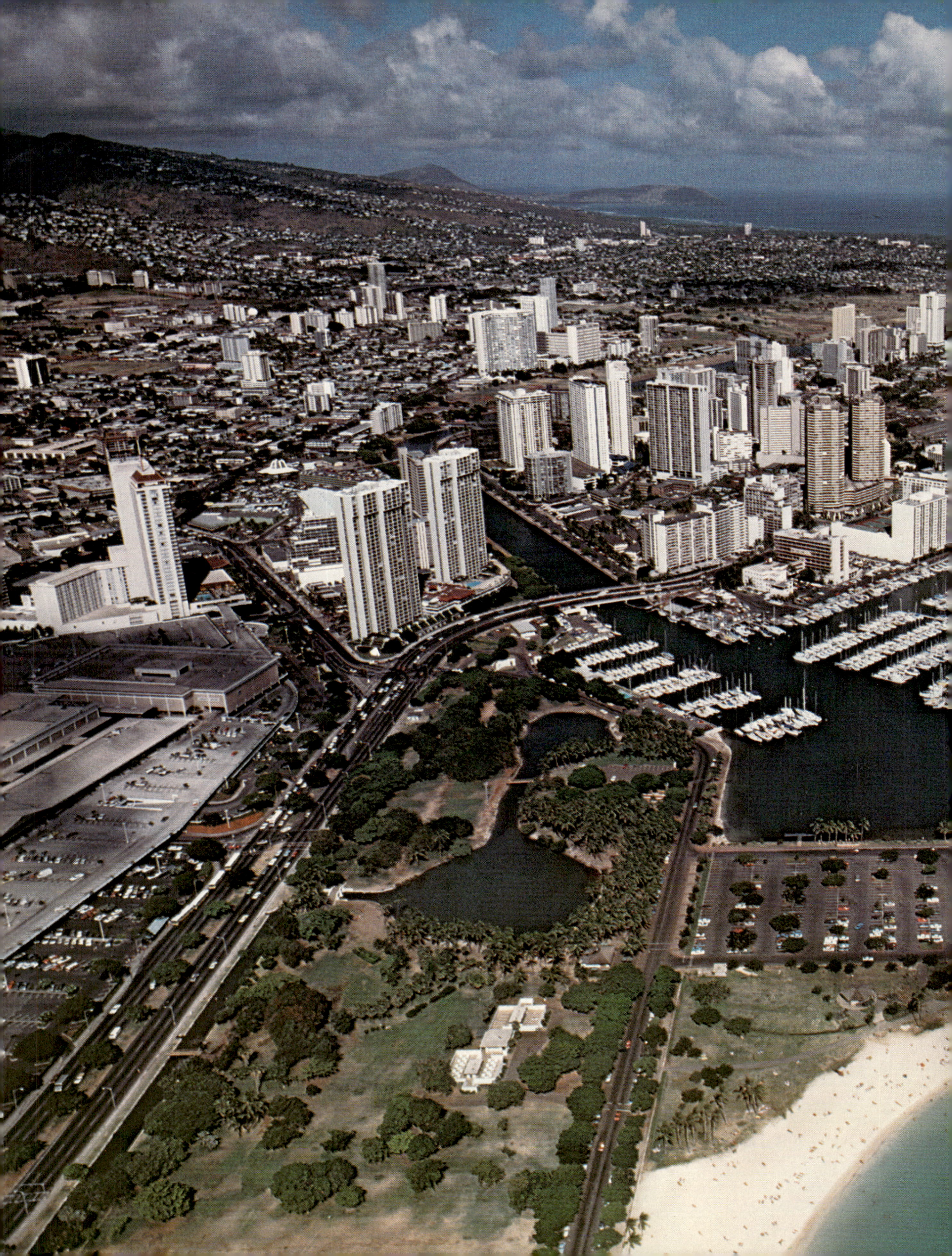

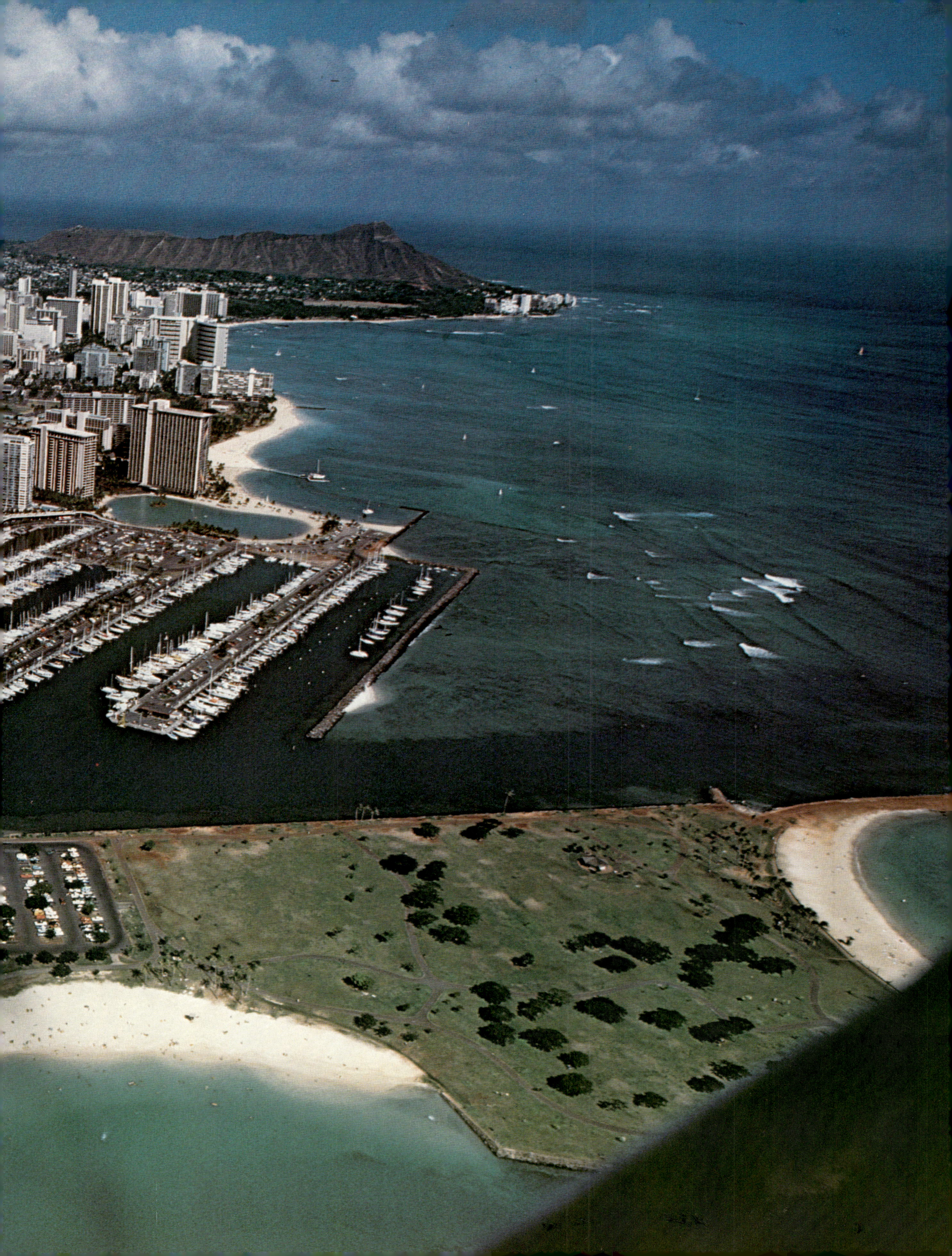

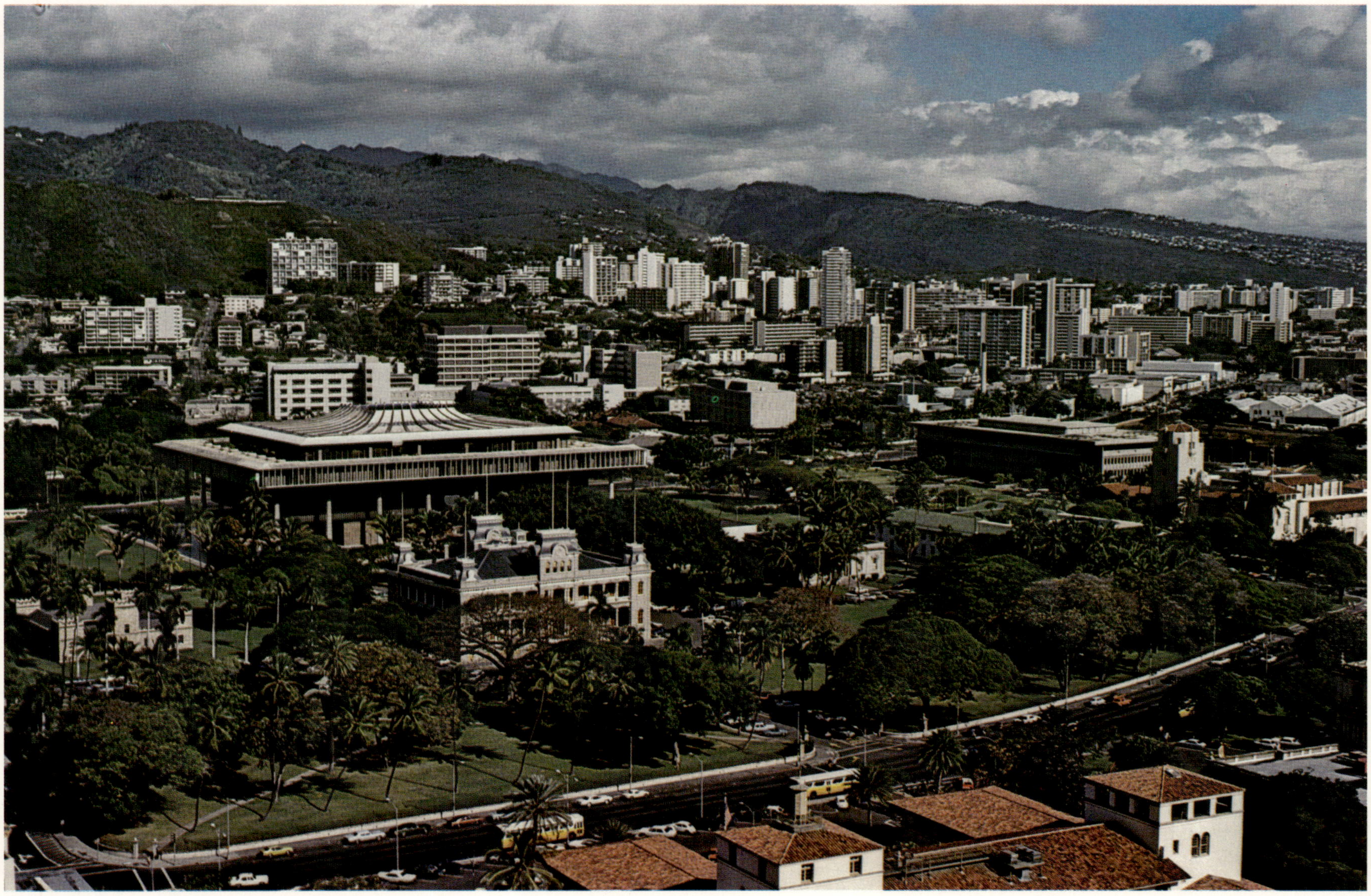

arrangement that seemed imminently fair to councilmen at the time, although they eventually switched to another chairman who was still anti-Fasi but wasn't running for anything. Fasi described the televised hearings as a "kangaroo court" and an attempt at political intimidation.

As testimony continued under TV lights, threats were allegedly made on the life of some witnesses, so the council hired armed bodyguards to protect them on a 24-hour basis. It didn't seem to matter that the private guard company had no business license and the guards no permits to carry guns. The public hearings dragged on for several months until the council decided nothing to anyone's satisfaction, turned over its files to the governor, and returned to its normal activity of granting zoning variances.

In the meantime, Fasi won reelection for mayor by a landslide, beating the council chairman and everyone else, and made it obvious he would next run for governor. At this time the state decided to enter the fray and Attorney General Ronald Amemiya hauled the principals into court, charging Fasi. When asked about his interest in the action, Governor George Ariyoshi said he had nothing to do with this turn of events, claiming in numerous interviews that he had never talked to his attorney general about Fasi, and the fact that he might be running for reelection for governor against Fasi was just a coincidence. On the same day the state's indictment was returned, Fasi, never one to be upstaged, answered the charges by announcing his candidacy for the governorship.

The actual trial was many months in starting, because of numerous preliminary motions of one kind or another, and attempts to remove witnesses or to grant them immunity. Just selecting the jury took weeks. The state's private prosecutor, hired from Los Angeles to take the proceedings "out of politics," didn't like the idea of people being on the jury who voted for Fasi, which proved difficult since Fasi had already won two elections in a row. Most jurors said they liked Fasi, but would be "fair" anyway. Dispositions by the dozens were collected by opposing attorneys, and Fasi himself often appeared in court on "vacation" time to observe proceedings. With daily front-page press coverage, nobody could say they hadn't heard anything, and it took as much as eight hours to screen a single juror, who was then often thrown out on preemptive options argued by one lawyer or another. The trial began after jurors had already been sequestered for two months.

It was clear that some kind of payments had been made, but were they just "campaign contributions" as Fasi claimed? Circuit Judge Toshimi Sodetani dismissed everything and went home, and so did the lawyer from Los Angeles. So, after almost two years, the Kukui Plaza Caper ended — and without a single word from Jack Lord. ■

No place can touch Honolulu. It has a great diversity of races and I think it has more harmony with all our multicultural people than any other place I have been in.

I live in Kailua. I have never minded the drive from Kailua over the pali to Honolulu. I always enjoy coming over the top of the hill and looking at the city and seeing how much it has grown since I have been here. There's been a tremendous growth in the last thirty-two years . . . I think I kind of basically liked it when it wasn't quite as large as it is. I'm kind of spoiled. I liked the Honolulu of thirty years ago better than I do today. I don't tend to be a city dweller. Basically I like the country. We moved to Kailua 25 or 30 years ago because it was a rural area. Now it is no longer rural.

Charles Clark, Superintendent
State Department of Education

Honolulu is a place where the people want to see and feel what they have heard and read and talked so much about.

Eileen Lota, City Clerk
City and County of Honolulu

Honolulu's civic center, the new state capitol, and Iolani Palace. Overleaf, the Hawaiian sunset colors Waikiki long before the hotel lights go on.

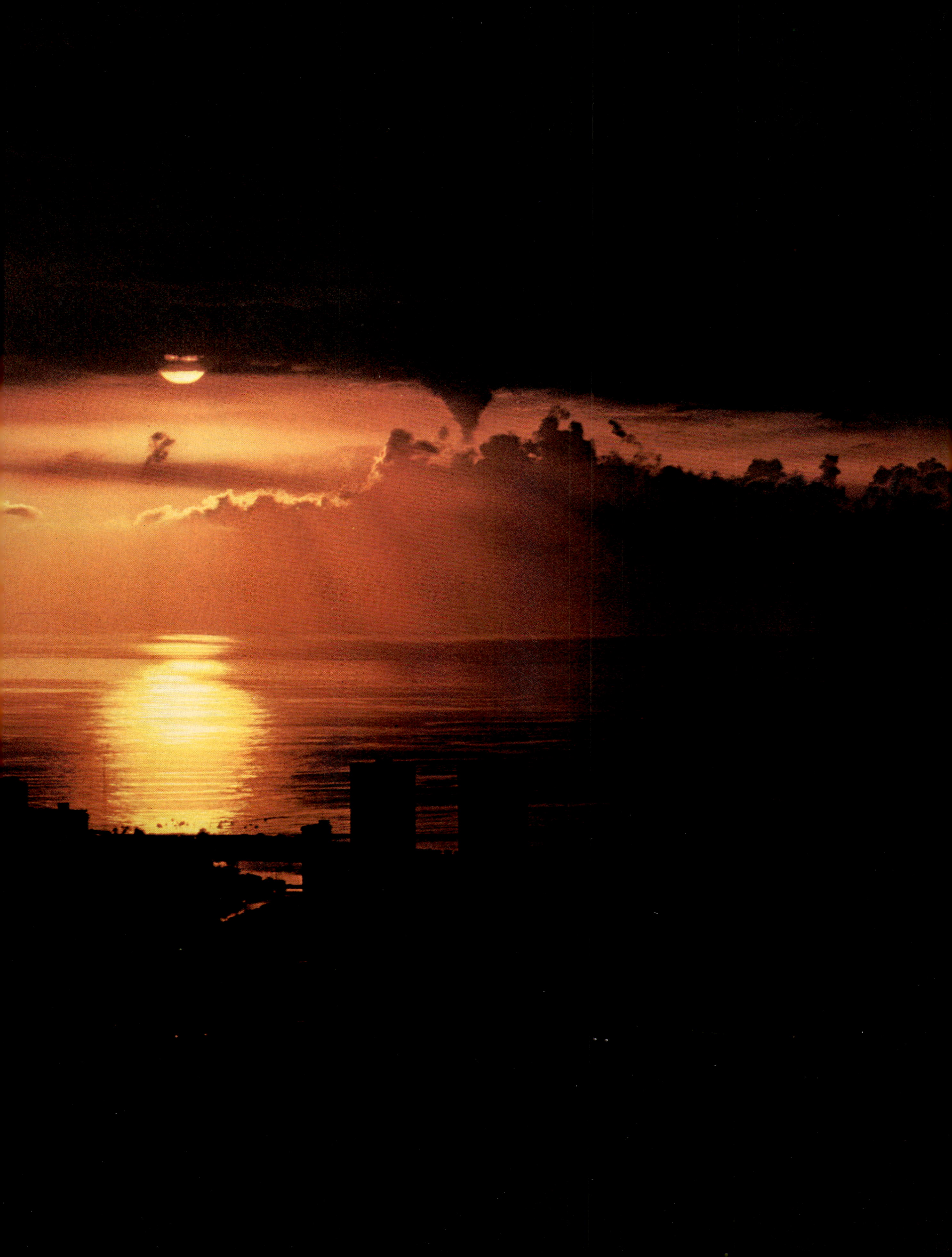

Honolulu Is Many Kinds of Living Places

Halfway around Oahu, as far as you can go without turning back, is Kahuku, an old sugar town now growing mostly seed corn and watermelons. The refurbished sugar mill is open to tourists, with the usual curio shops arrayed alongside. A paved parking lot accommodates round-the-island tour buses, whose drivers allow their passengers only enough time for the rest room and the mill tour.

Within sight of the tour bus passengers is a town they never see — the old Kahuku Sugar Company plantation camp, one of the last remaining sugar camps on Oahu. The narrow streets are still unpaved, the small houses whitewashed, and the tiny backyard vegetable gardens instant identification of the owner's nationality — they plant the ethnic food they eat. Crowing, fighting cocks betray the homes of gamblers, and the pungent odor of yellow pickled turnip will identify a first generation Japanese. In the fall, Boys Day is celebrated with a colorful red and blue paper carp flying in the wind. Far back here the dusty streets twist and bend, then widen to allow parking space in front of Owan's General Store, still open and selling. In the back is Tsuru's Restaurant and across the street is Helen's Barber Shop, not far from a weathered, gray Buddhist temple.

Kahuku Camp is far away from Waikiki in time, distance, and standard of living — still another facet of the cosmopolitan flavor of Honolulu as a city and island. The city is like a skein of multicolored yarn, with unknown colors gradually being uncovered as the round-the-island bus passes remote beach resorts, strip developments crowding the road, plantation towns, military housing, and expensive residential neighborhoods creeping up narrow ridges into the hills. It is a kaleidoscope variety of places to live fitting every pocketbook and style.

Mililani town, probably Honolulu's newest neighborhood, sits squarely in the center of what were once Dole pineapple fields. Waipahu's new residential areas are old C & H sugar cane fields, and many *mauka* Kaneʻohe subdivisions cover banana farms that were reluctantly given up by their owners. Only Makakilo above Barbers Point is built where nothing was before.

On the windward side long, strip communities fill in the narrow plots remaining between the *pali* and the beach. Some beach homes are perched clear of the ground on poles, permitting high waves to pass through without washing the house away. The posted warnings of "High Surf Area" and "Tsunami Evacuation Road" have particularly significant meaning along the shore at Kaʻaʻawa, Punaluʻu and Hauʻula, where 30-foot-high "tidal waves" swept inland on April Fools' day in 1946.

Sea Life Park, Makapuʻu.

Well, I've seen a lot of changes. A lot of people complain about all this brick and mortar, but, I don't know, it's still home to me. It means a lot to me. They talk about planning. I don't know. There is a certain amount of planning you've got to do, but there has to be some uniqueness to your local situation that makes something out of it. A good example of that is Kona — Kailua Kona. It probably has the least amount of planning and yet people like it and want to go there and it's growing. It's still a very quaint place. I was in Australia last year, in Canberra. Now there's a planned city and it is the most cold and sterile city I've ever seen. I don't like it.

John Bellinger, President
First Hawaiian Bank

The rapid population growth of Honolulu on limited island land has resulted in continuous changes in land use, at times causing destructive alteration in the landscape, as well as traumatic displacement of people, and in some areas, eradication of traditional rural land uses. Modern developments have sometimes been imposed rather harshly upon the island.

The ancient Hawaiian mullet ponds at Kuapa near Koko Crater were dredged by industrialist Henry Kaiser into the Hawaii Kai complex of marinas and townhouses that continue to expand in all directions. Fifteen years ago there were only fish, *kiawe* trees, and pig farms in Maunalua Valley.

When Kaiser first moved into Maunalua and Kalama, the pig farmers and newly arrived counter-culture people joined in an effort to preserve the small farms and rural lifestyle they enjoyed at low rents on old Bishop Estate leaseholds. The farmers lost, but only after staging a sit-in in front of the bulldozers. Police dragged them away as they pleaded for the right to live on the land that Hawaiian Princess Bernice Pauahi Bishop inherited from their ancestors, land that Bishop Estate trustees had now leased to Kaiser.

I had previously struggled with Kaiser myself as land use commissioner, and in the process we grew to know each other well. Kaiser first started in business as a studio photographer, and he often took time from his busy schedule to proudly show me his early photographs when I called at his office. I tried to convince him that a little mix of people and occupations in the vast development at Hawaii Kai would be very desirable. I also tried my best to keep his houses off the dramatic ridges around Kuapa Pond, but to no avail. He was a very stubborn man.

When I tried to convince my fellow commissioners to deny urban zoning for the narrow ridges and for Oahu's south shore beyond the Blowhole, Kaiser personally drove himself downtown to the Land Use Commission office and, with his associates waiting hesitantly in the hallway, loudly expressed his extreme displeasure at a public zoning body that would deny him the right to do anything he wanted with his land. Kaiser said he would sue me, and he threatened to abandon the entire multimillion-dollar Hawaii Kai project unless he immediately received permission to subdivide Kalama Valley and build on every ridge. The "progress" and growth-oriented commission members quickly retreated, and I was unable to muster sufficient votes to prevent Kaiser from receiving almost everything he demanded. He never consulted with the small farmers and Hawaiian families living deep inside Kalama Valley. The zoning change was decided by Kaiser.

As so often happens in Hawaii, the struggle between Kaiser and myself fostered a lasting friendship. I was the only photographer to photograph his home on Koko Head, where he lived until his death, when Hawaii Kai was still in early stages of construction. We would ride off together in his pink jeep to watch his pink bulldozers and pink landmovers rearrange Maunalua land. Even his dredge and tugboats were pink. His "Five Companies" built Boulder Dam on the Colorado River and a Liberty ship a day during World War II. He was one of the many immigrants to Hawaii who substantially changed the shape of things.

There was a stir of political reaction to Kaiser's confrontation with the farmers, causing legislators to debate a bill recognizing the existence of semisubsistence farming in a rural environment. Senator Nadao Yoshinaga called for a study of population stabilization in a racially and economically mixed community, which would recognize the prior rights of people living on the land. He wanted consideration of individually styled communities appropriate to counter-culture lifestyles of people who want to live on the land in their own way in hand-built structures exempt from conventional building codes. The bill was defeated by a legislative majority that would have none of this rural lifestyle nonsense.

The erection of personal "country-style" homes without regard to expensive zoning restrictions and building codes has been difficult to halt on Oahu, where isolated valleys and wooded land along the shore support many

---

We got to restrict the population and tourists to certain numbers. You can't let them grow hog wild. If we imposed ourselves on San Francisco or Los Angeles and over-populated their space they'd call a halt to it. So, I think the Governor has got a good idea. We've got to watch it. So far so good. Certainly the islands haven't suffered from these tourists, but when it gets out of hand you gotta prepare for it . . . They have these conventions all the time. We shouldn't go out and solicit these conventions. Let 'em get down on their knees to come to Hawaii. Let them start begging a little bit. Then we can be a bit choosy.

Vernon "Red" McQueen
Sports writer

hidden shacks that building inspectors have never seen. Some who do have permits constructed innovative dwellings and plain single-walled cottages on unpaved roads in remote areas where water is still collected off the roof to make the inside plumbing work. The need for concrete sidewalks is hardly necessary for bare feet.

The building department ordered a beach shack in Wai'anae torn down because no building permit had been obtained and it claimed the structure was not safe. The inspector said, "They have to follow the same kind of construction as conventional building construction. By that I mean they have to use nails. They can't hold it together with ropes." The Hawaiian grass shack is apparently no longer acceptable at City Hall.

Hawaiian families living on small semisubsistance farms in Waikane-Waiahole valleys are still struggling to prevent their valleys from being converted into expensive rural subdivisions. They like low rents and don't object to unpaved roads. When adjacent Kahana Valley was purchasd for a state park and eviction notices posted to allow "proper development" of the park for public use, families in the valley successfully halted their ouster. Lydia Dela Cerra, speaking for the park families, said, "This valley has housed our ancestors for many, many years. Isn't it a privilege that we, the offspring of Hawaiian ancestry, should be given rights to remain in the valley which once held the *mana* of the natives here, which is slowly dispersing into thin air?"

"We love our land," said her neighbor in the next valley. "We also love our ancestors, and we cannot and will not see them ripped out of the land by bulldozers. They kill a little bit of us every time they take our land."

The Hawaiians have now gone to Congress to get back the land they claim is rightfully theirs. They ask for "compensation for losses resulting from the overthrow of the Hawaiian Kingdom." They want one billion dollars, plus title to all federal lands in Hawaii that become surplus to government needs. A congressional commission has been appointed to study methods of possible compensation to native Hawaiians for their lost lands. Their attorney adds that the claim is just as valid as the settlement recently received by Alaskan Indians and Eskimos.

The Hui Malama 'Aina Ko'olau, a Hawaiian community organization, says they do not pretend to stop development, but with their race nearing extinction and so few pure-blooded Hawaiians remaining, they do ask to participate in the decisions that shape their future and their land. "We demand that it be development that builds on the life of the people," says Hui Malama, "that preserves our values and that nourishes the children of all the native people of Hawaii. We cannot any more allow development that destroys the things that make Hawaii what it is." ∎

In crime statistics the local population is broken down into its respective components. Caucasians are, as always, lumped into one category without distinction as to ethnic background ... It's high time that people here realize that ethnic identity is not limited to "minority groups" like Korean, Samoan, Chinese, and that Irish, Germans, Italians, French et. al. have backgrounds as diverse and valuable as any other group ... To be honest, I find this whole ethnic breakdown business to be utterly valueless and grossly distracting from the fact that we are all fellow human beings, but if it is to be done to one group, why not for all? ... Who's kidding whom? Are we to continue with the divisive nonsense or are we finally going to wake up to the fact that we're all just people? Ethnic identity is fine when it includes all, but all too often it obscures our common identity and is used to fuel the fire of racism.

Gregory Shepherd, Kailua
English teacher

This community is the kind of place where I can really affirm the doctrine of creation.

Bishop Edmond Browning
Episcopal Diocese, Honolulu

A tropical fruit stand at Kahalu'u invites buyers in shoes or bare feet.

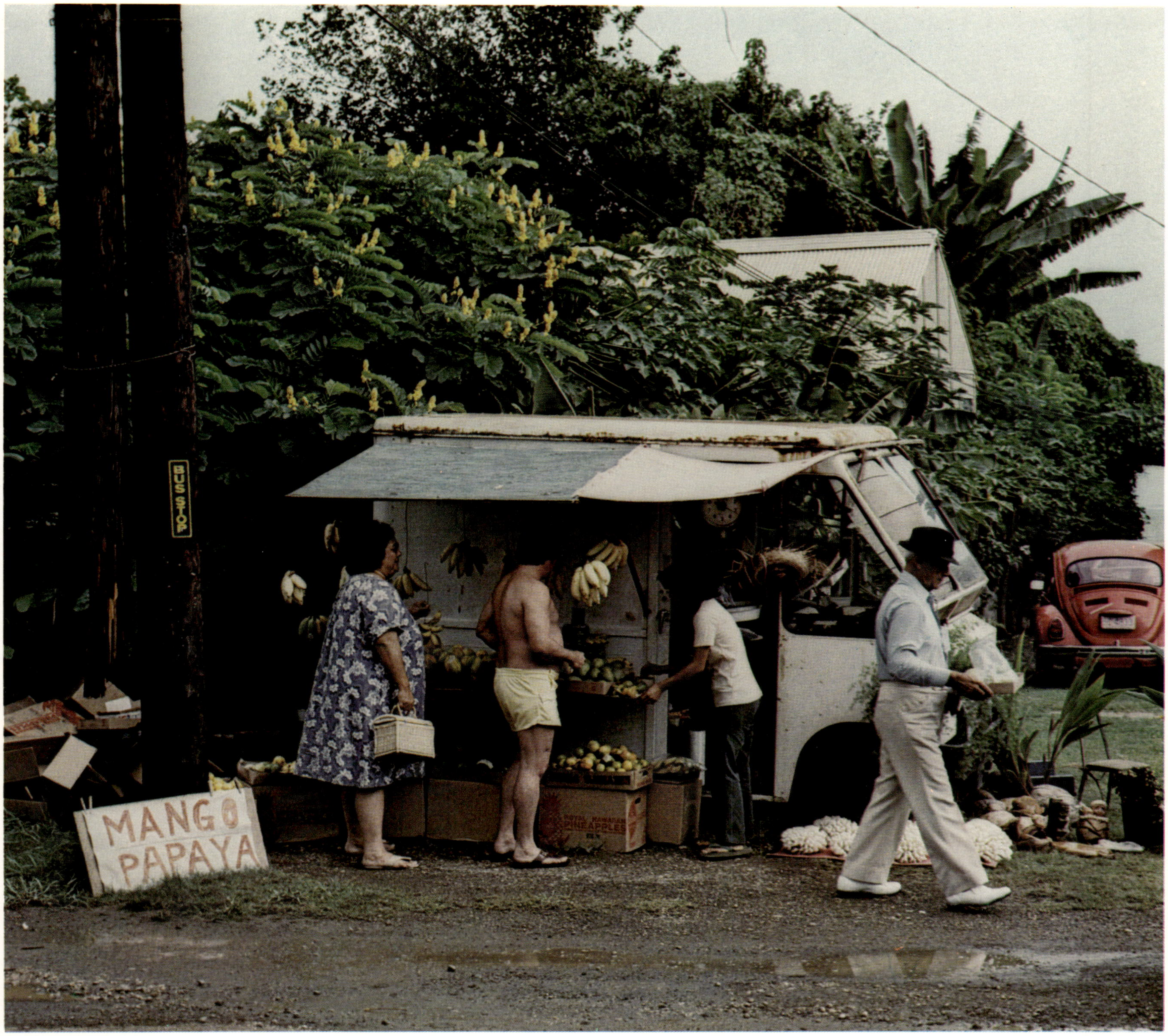
BUS STOP
MANGO
PAPAYA
PINEAPPLES

The Aloha Spirit Is Not A Myth

In January, Japanese *tofu* makers take alternating two-week vacations so there will always be *tofu* on supermarket shelves. Of course, not everyone does this; the Kewalo pickle factory took just one week's vacation last year, and it was long enough for fresh bottled pickles to disappear. I drove into a service station in Kaneʻohe town, giving the usual request, "Fill 'er up," only to hear the candidly honest Hawaiian attendant tell me, "I'm all out of super. I forgot to order." I'll always remember my visit to a hotel gift shop, where I inquired why my paper-cover book, *Kauai*, was not in stock. The pretty clerk told me my book was a lot of trouble, because it was always selling out and she had to reorder!

Honolulu is that place where the world goes by outside while we "do our own 'ting," as it is said in local pidgin, and ignore what is considered normal elsewhere. Our relaxed and kindly attitude has successfully resisted brutalization despite plantation *lunas*, politicians, and war. We are nice to each other and kindly to strangers. With all our troubles (and we do have troubles) the people of Hawaii have remained alive and vibrant. The "aloha spirit" is not a myth.

Spanish galleons carrying plundered gold from Manila to Acapulco sailed within less than a hundred miles from the islands. If our consistant, year-round trade winds had changed ever so slightly, we would be speaking Spanish today. Now there is serious discussion in political chambers on how to maintain our traditional ethnic balance of Oriental, Polynesian, and *haole* to prevent Honolulu from becoming mostly *haole* like all the other states. We don't want to lose what we have, but we're not quite sure how to keep it.

One of the problems involved in maintaining cultural integrity is knowing what you have, but in many specific areas we don't know what it is. I wouldn't know how to inventory ethnic assets, and I know it would be impossible — and unwise — to determine what the best racial combination is. Our life modes and way with people can easily be exported — our philosophy and people relationships taken home as souvenirs — and we should encourage spreading the message far and wide. It is perhaps the most valuable commodity anyone can possess, and it is free. The visitor can look at our scenery, but must not touch. They can take away everything else, because we have lots of good living.

For those concerned about Hawaii's growth rate, this book is a disaster — now everyone will want to live here! It is truly a dilemma. When people telephone me in Honolulu, I generally tell them it is raining and has been for the past week. (Actually, to a certain extent this is true, because it rains almost every night in the mountains back of Manoa. Upper Manoa Valley averages about 90 inches a year — this is more than monsoon weather in central India.) Perhaps this might discourage a few. But I know it doesn't rain all the time. I can only write a book about a very wonderful place and hope the philosophy behind it all is exportable — a lifestyle that visitors can emulate and take back home. Perhaps we can be copied in every detail in other places.

We are reminded by every decision that scars the earth or our people that we must live on earth's terms. If we want a beautiful island — a livable island forever, with a remunerative economy in future years — we must make it so by rational and thoughtful decisions based on nature's restrictive terms — not ours. Even planning for so-called "controlled growth" is meaningless if there is no actual limit. The carrying capacity of the island is determined by our needs for open space, clean air, agriculture, and places to live, eat, and enjoy, and these needs must be the determinant of the island's optimum population. Over the short term we can grow fat and rich if we wish to duplicate Las Vegas; but in the process we will destroy our way of living and our island in the sun.

Please understand the need to tread gently upon our island. We cannot build a hotel on every beach or a condominium apartment on every hillside. There is only room for so many people at a time, and when we are full, some will have to wait their turn. If we allow entry to all visitors who are able to afford a ticket, our unique island treasure may be lost — to everyone. Please understand if sometimes the people of Honolulu occasionally must advise, "No more reservations are available — the island is full." ∎

Honolulu is the example I hope someday all America will follow . . . it's the Aloha spirit we have — no other place has it.

Charles Clark, Superintendent
State Department of Education

King Kamehameha draped in plumeria flower *leis* on his birthday celebration. The original statue was lost at sea on its way to Honolulu from its Italian sculptor. This is the second.

Kualoa on Kaneʻohe Bay.

Dedicated to my Honolulu children:
    Tad Miki
    Jay Koki
    Miyo Nancy
    Chiye Rana